LIFE WITHOUT

Tatiana Shcherbina was born in Moscow. Before 1999 she worked on Radio Liberty and four of her collections of poems were published in *samizdat*. Since 1999 she has published six volumes of poetry and prose in Russia and two volumes of poetry in French, her adopted mother tongue. She has been a journalist and reviewer for a number of the Russian broadsheets and her articles and poems have also appeared in French newspapers. In 2002 she took part in Poetry International at the Royal Festival Hall and a UK-wide tour of Russian women poets. Her poems have appeared in *In the Grip of Strange Thoughts: Russian Poetry in a New Era*, edited by J. Kates (Bloodaxe Books, UK; Zephyr Press, USA, 1999) and in *Modern Poetry in Translation 20: Russian Women's Poetry*, edited by Valentina Polukhina (2002), and a selection from her early work, *The Score of the Game*, translated by J. Kates, was published in the USA by Zephyr Press in 2003. *Life Without: Selected Poetry & Prose 1992-2003*, translated by Sasha Dugdale (Bloodaxe Books, 2004), is her first book to be published in Britain.

Sasha Dugdale is a translator and consultant for the Royal Court Theatre. Her translations include *Black Milk and Plasticine* by Vassily Sigarev (Evening Standard Most Promising Playwright Award) and *Terrorism* by the Presnyakov Brothers. Her first collection of poems *Notebook* was published by Carcanet/OxfordPoets in 2003. She received an Eric Gregory Award for that collection in 2003.

TATIANA SHCHERBINA

Life Without

SELECTED POETRY & PROSE
1992–2003

translated by
SASHA DUGDALE

BLOODAXE BOOKS

Copyright © Tatiana Shcherbina 2004
English translation © Sasha Dugdale 2004

ISBN: 1 85224 642 1

First published 2004 by
Bloodaxe Books Ltd,
Highgreen,
Tarset,
Northumberland NE48 1RP.

www.bloodaxebooks.com
For further information about Bloodaxe titles
please visit our website or write to
the above address for a catalogue.

Bloodaxe Books Ltd acknowledges
the financial assistance of
Arts Council England, North East.

Cover printing by J. Thomson Colour Printers Ltd, Glasgow.

Printed in Great Britain by
Cromwell Press Ltd, Trowbridge, Wiltshire.

СОДЕРЖАНИЕ

CONTENTS

FOREWORD

The poems and prose in this collection are almost all from the 1990s, the period after Perestroika when the USSR collapsed and Russia became, at least nominally, a free-market state and a democracy. It was a time of rapid change and upheaval in Russia and much of this change was focused on the capital Moscow. It is worth beginning a discussion of context here because Tatiana Shcherbina is from Moscow and identifies very strongly with the capital city. In her essay on the history of Moscow she writes that Russia's size and shifting borders make it impossible for her to know the country or feel anything for it: she is a Muscovite.

Moscow became in a very short time one of the wealthiest cities in the world. Its skyline was altered overnight as hundreds of new office and apartment blocks sprung up, roads were resurfaced and the whole city became an advertising hoarding for glamorous new imported products. Moscow was also the reluctant host to two attempted coups and became a notoriously unsafe city. Whilst some profited immensely from regime change a growing class of Muscovites found themselves destitute and helpless. As nowhere else in Russia, the very rich and the very poor lived side by side, often in the same blocks.

These were the facts that made the headlines in Europe during the 1990s: violence, social upheaval and dislocation, extreme poverty. However, there was also a growing group of people who were affected by change but managed to stay afloat, to survive, and even to make use of the freedoms the new Russia offered: the opportunity to travel abroad cheaply – to Europe, the Mecca of the Russian intelligentsia, and to the Mediterranean on package tours and cruises. New economic freedoms meant that a proud bourgeoisie could emerge and a real frenzy of home improvement and car buying began. In fact Russia is possibly the only European country in which the intelligentsia espouse defiantly bourgeois ideals and – possibly in reaction to the years of Communism – almost Thatcherite economic beliefs. By the beginning of the 21st century a sense of optimism prevailed. Russia seemed to have reached a degree of economic and political stability and this group of new bourgeois Russians felt themselves justified in their belief that they deserved a certain standard of living.

There are references to this new consumer lifestyle everywhere in Shcherbina's prose and poems. In the essay 'Craze' she examines the Russian "boom" mentality: all the country is suddenly buying new household appliances in the way that they used to be discussing a certain theatre performance. In the same piece she looks at the way that the prices of real estate in Moscow have brought an end to the great Russian tradition of hoarding. She does not heap scorn on these new consumer habits as Western commentators often do.

For Tatiana Shcherbina these social phenomena need to be explained and recorded and not judged. Besides she makes it clear that the negative aspects of the changes in Russia, Wild West capitalism and consumerism, deprivation and suffering are worth enduring because of the new freedom of expression: 'But for all that – freedom and the freedom to choose: to say and do as you please.' The poems often detail the appearance of new appliances and new technology – there is a proliferation of faxes, printers, computers, scanners, telephones and a whole poem devoted to the new virtual Russia, Runet. Perhaps as no other Russian poet Shcherbina has charted the consumerism of a new Russian lifestyle.

Tatiana Shcherbina was an established poet before Perestroika. Four of her collections were published in *samizdat* and circulated unofficially. She participated actively in underground or what she terms 'second' culture, but is adamant that she was not a dissident – just not an officially acceptable writer. Perhaps it is in part this neutrality which has enabled her to continue writing and flourish in the difficult transitional period after Perestroika. The arts in Russia underwent profound change during the 1990s. Dissidents found themselves without an enemy and without a cause, party-affiliated individuals and establishments died a quiet death or re-established themselves with a new image, and artists and writers gained a bewildering new freedom to do as they pleased. Much of the 90s was spent trying to find an inheritance and a sense of purpose and continuity in the arts.

It is a commonly held view that the 70 years of Communism were an aberration and that artists and writers are best served by going back to the pre-revolutionary models – witness the extreme popularity of Akunin's detective novels, set in the 19th century, and now translated into English. The rejection of political and socially motivated writing and art has lead to a rise in the popularity of art which is extremely personal and stresses the internal life and plight of the individual and also a proliferation of art "for art's sake", decorative and decadent art.

The range of new preoccupations and directions has been matched by an array of new publishing ventures, from glossy periodicals to philosophical tracts, and publishing is vigorous, if at times sporadic and varying in quality. This, however, has offered writers the chances to practise different media. A number of well-known writers have become frequent contributors to newspapers, glossy magazines and radio programmes and Shcherbina is no exception to this. Her prose is published widely in the Russian press and she worked for some time at Radio Liberty. Her poetry has been published by a range of smaller independent presses, often affiliated with poetry venues, such as the Moscow-based O.G.I. Press.

Contact with non-Russian art and literature has undoubtedly influenced Russian writers and artists. At first the influx of foreign films and translations, exhibitions and theatres was wholeheartedly welcomed. But as the 90s progressed the reception of foreign culture in Russia became a barometer of national esteem. Whenever Russia felt itself to be embattled it looked to "Russian" culture for consolation and rejected various manifestations of the foreign culture. Yet the fact remains that Russian contemporary culture has drawn extensively from external sources, both to redress the balance after 70 years of near isolation, and to continue the search for models and influences beyond the discredited Soviet ones.

Tatiana Shcherbina has occupied an enviable position: she lived in Paris for part of the 90s, learnt fluent French and even began writing poems and articles in French. Her comments on European culture are fascinating because she has direct experience of this culture (despite the increase in travel abroad relatively few Russians have a profound knowledge of a European culture) and she writes for Russians who do not know Europe as she does, but who are captivated by the European 'exotic'. Her poems and prose are filled with European place names, characters and habits. In 'Why I don't live in Paris' she explains the attraction of Paris, but comments that her Russian roots force her to return to Russia.

She is a Russian at heart, her Russianness cannot be understood by the French and so she must return to her own country. Tatiana Shcherbina's patriotism may seem quaint or odd to us – try substituting Russian with British in this essay – but it must be placed in context. Russians are eager to find themselves in this bewildering new order. They no longer have to define themselves as Soviet socialist citizens and there is both the intellectual freedom to explore identity and a certain amount of external pressure to do so.

The question of national identity crops up frequently as Russia comes to terms with a disintegrating empire and waves of immigration from former Soviet republics. Debates about national character are common and the 1990s were characterised by a rise in Russian Orthodox belief, Russian patriotism and crude nationalism. 'Russianness' is as much a topic for art and literature as it is for conversation in Russia. An interest in personal identity is often linked with this: writers will frequently trace their family history, the history of their 'clan' back to a period when the issue of national and personal identity was less fraught. Of course the use of family history as subject-matter for literature is not limited to Russia, but there is far more at stake in Russia. Much of Shcherbina's prose is concerned with this quest for genealogical history. In the essays 'August' and 'The Family Unit' she describes with nostalgic tenderness a gathering at the dacha before death and quarrelling divided the family. A Villeroy and Boch tea pot stand which she still possesses represents both pre-revolutionary links with Europe and a continuity with a real Russian genealogical unit: 'Here it is, the stand. It's almost the only evidence that I once belonged to a family unit which had survived from the creation of the world right up to our time.'

Tatiana Shcherbina has been frequently criticised by her compatriots for being negative about Russia – a curious indication of how important national feeling is in Russia. Certainly she is never one-sided. Compare the poem 'Dictatorship, democracy...' for example with her pride at the rebirth of Moscow or the way the Russian women look more French than the French. She describes Russia with the detached irony of a foreigner, possibly because of the time she has spent abroad, possibly because, as a member of the Moscow intelligentsia, the rest of Russia is very distant to her. 'The majority of the Russian nation,' according to Shcherbina, 'had no need for freedom and found inequality unacceptable. It is freedom itself, which makes this majority aggressive and helpless, and the whip which makes it obedient. Moscow is the exception to this.' The divide between the urban intelligentsia and the masses in Russia is as wide as it ever has been and new economic and social freedoms have had little impact in bridging this divide.

Russia was and remains a patriarchal society and Russian women do not have the equality European and American women enjoy. Domestic duties, for example, are almost always carried out by women in Russia. (It is worth pointing out that a new generation of urban women who have careers and active lives manage this with the help of their older female relatives.) Numbers of gender stereotypes exist and myths about the sexes are prevalent: most Russian women will claim a femininity and womanliness which their European sisters have 'lost' in their quest for equality. The division between 'nun' and 'whore', made in the famous Soviet condemnation of the poet Anna Akhmatova as 'half-nun, half-whore', is still a working division in the Russian perception of women, and women's sexual emancipation is achieved often at the cost of security and stability. Tatiana Shcherbina's essay on the history of Moscow looks back to a time in the 1980s when a more relaxed political regime coincided with a spate of passionate affairs – but it seems certain that women had more to lose than the men. In her poems the persona of the jilted and sexually disappointed lover is a common one and the fear of being left to age alone is present in a number of the poems. The only defence is a strident femininity – a barrage of make-up, perfume and heels.

Russian poetry is a very male domain in this very male country. There are still relatively few women poets and the majority of these write in a style and with preoccupations which are deemed 'feminine' – love, personal relationships, disappointment in love. There appears to be considerable reluctance to take on more universal issues. However Tatiana Shcherbina uses the jilted and disappointed woman lover to draw together a number of themes: the theme of ageing and unfulfilled dreams and ambitions underpins the disappointment at a failed relationship. In her prose she states this explicitly. The character of Lena in the piece 'August' makes it clear that life foists the unwanted upon you, that you notice your earlier dreams have been thwarted only when it is too late. In poems such as 'The helplessness of a bee...' or 'I'm missing something. What it is I don't know...' the conclusion of the poem is a realisation that all the choices are made, the borders closed. The only respite, or counterbalance to this pessimism is the image of a golden childhood and the love and protection of parents and grandparents.

In a number of the poems the loneliness and disappointment of the lyrical voice is projected onto the outside world: the fragmented and isolating new capitalist society of the 90s. In 'Won't I ever see you again...' the lover's sacrifice is described in terms of the new economic realities: 'I paid the very highest rate: / my life, round here they call it: *cash*.' Shcherbina uses the English word 'cash' in the original – a new slang word for money in Russian. In 'Spring Conscription', a poem which plays on the yearly Russian conscription of new recruits, she compares the new slang words which have appeared in Russian with her own band of words: 'dreariness, protest, pointers adrift'. The new words dodge conscription (an ironic reference to the ease with which many recruits do dodge conscription) and their linguistic duty: defending a past world which had words of greater emotional depth and value than the superficial new slang additions to the Russian language.

Several poems are set in the warren-like Moscow flats, where one can be at once quite alone and very close to thousands of other people, and it is this proximity which reminds the speaker how alone she is – it is only a 'neighbour's snored lullaby' which sends her to sleep after a night tapping away at the computer. In the poem 'They've turned off all the hot water...' the reality of the hot water being switched off (an annual occurrence in Russia) becomes a metaphor for the absence of love. In later poems, such as 'Bed', the themes are much wider – terrorism, the clash of fundamentalist religions, the arrogance of European thinking – but these are again seen through the prism of the bedroom and 'the slightly crumpled world of bed'.

So far I have offered a wider context for the poetry and prose in this collection. I wanted to finish by briefly considering Tatiana Shcherbina's poetic style. Perhaps what is most striking about her poetry in the original Russian is the density of wordplay, allusion and quotation. Even poems which are ostensibly about loss of love often have a linguistic ebullience which belies their message. Song titles, cultural references and proverbs are woven into the poetry and often the motivation for the poem seems to be the creative potential of the language itself. Wherever possible I have tried to find equivalent English quotations, proverbs and references, but I have been mindful of the need to retain the Russianness of the poetry and Tatiana Shcherbina's allusions. She also mixes various tones and registers in Russia, using slang, archaisms, proper nouns, foreign words and expletives and shifting between them with a bewildering speed. It is difficult to recreate this effect in the English without overloading the poem – perhaps because many of the linguistic barriers and formalities which she dismantles in her work no longer exist in English poetry, where shifting register and language has long been a feature.

I have tried to retain the formal and rhythmical qualities of Tatiana Shcherbina's poetry. But like most contemporary Russian poets, she uses rhyme in almost all of her poetry, and this is neither desirable, nor possible in English.

In recent collections Shcherbina has moved to a style which she describes as 'New Sincerity'. In poems from later collections written between 1997 and 2001 she uses a purer, pared down language to describe an emotional state. These are well represented here because they are less altered in translation.

The prose collected here is a representative sample. It includes pieces chosen to offer some context and background for the poetry, such as 'The History of Moscow', 'August' and 'Why I don't live in Paris'; examples of more philosophical essays, 'Light' and 'Transparency'; and a series of short pieces of poetic prose commissioned by the Pushkin Museum of Fine Arts for an exhibition on Jan Komensky. These pieces were exhibited at the museum alongside pieces of art by contemporary Russian artists.

SASHA DUGDALE

ACKNOWLEDGEMENTS

The poetry and prose in this selection is drawn from the following Russian editions: *Lazurnaya Skrizhal'* (O.G.I., 2003), *Zhizn' Bez* (Biblioteka Zhurnala "Zolotoi Vek", 1997) and *Kniga o...* (Mitin Zhurnal, 2001); some new, uncollected work is also included.

Special thanks are due to Arts Council England for providing a translation grant for this book, and to the South Bank Centre for help with the translations by Sasha Dugdale, many of which were read for the first time in the UK at Poetry International 2002.

SELECTED POETRY

Жизнь без тебя

Жизнь без тебя заброшенна, убога,
недорога и просто недотрога,
кошмарносонна как ларек в Ельце,
продорогнута в холодном пальтеце,
бесчувственна, безаппеляционна,
и страшный суд, вершимый каждый миг —
лишь скучная мичуринская зона,
где степь да степь да друг степей калмык.
К чему ни прививайся, к розе или
к советскому дичку,
я всё как лошадь, загнанная в мыле
под стать качку,
который бицепс воли накачает
и терпит вновь
жизнь без тебя, в раздоре и печали,
моя любовь.

Life without you

Life without you is neglected, ramshackle,
cheap and simply unapproachable,
nightmarish like a provincial grocer's shack,
frozen through in a light summer mac,
without feeling, without right of appeal,
and judgment day, every second signed and sealed,
is boring botanist's countryside,
where the steppe is endless and the lone horseman rides.
Whatever I'm grafted onto – the rose
or the wild Soviet fruit-giver,
I'm always the horse, driven till it foams,
a match for the bodybuilder,
who builds up the biceps of self-will
and endures over and over
life without you, in discord, despair,
my lover.

[1996]

К Аполлону

Мне правды интуиция не скажет:
она пристрастна, ей глаза слепит,
автоответчик Бога - тоже лажа,
я оставляла тысячи молитв.
Речь прошлого я слышу внутривенно,
и ультразвуком колет мне в боку
всю ночь: дала обет молчанья Вена
и только лыко тычет мне в строку.
Ни время, ни места не изменили
мне памяти: проснуться как на взлет
лишь оттого, что по утрам - любили.
Теперь же сила воли мной встает.

Где только я забвенья ни искала:
на родине летающих слонов,
в краю верблюдов, где растут нахалы
(арабский - "пальмы"). Вот в стране богов
об остров Аполлона греюсь робко -
мне здесь в подошву вставили мозоль.
Колосс Родосский, будь моей раскопкой,
я брызжу просьбой, как аэрозоль!
Чудесный Аполлоша, муз водитель,
стихом тебе любезнее заход,
так вот: пошли мне поворот событий
классический, где клик - и повезет.

To Apollo

My intuition won't tell me the truth:
it's biased, they've blinded its eyes.
God's answer phone is crap as well,
I've left thousands of prayers.
I hear the past's speech intravenously,
it gives me a stitch in ultrasound
all night: Vienna vowed silence,
but points out when I've not saved nine.
Neither time nor place have failed
my memory: I wake up like I'm flying...
Only because we made love in the morning,
now willpower alone gets me going.

I've looked for oblivion everywhere:
The land of the airborne elephant;
camel country, where the palms grow
with Arabic names, now in the gods' land
I'm warming myself gently on Apollo's Isle –
where I found blisters on my sole.
Colossus of Rhodes, let me unearth you,
I spray my request like an aerosol!
Apollo baby, the Muses' Master,
I send you in verse the sunset of sunsets,
so hear: I want a classical turn of events,
where supplication meets with success.

[1997]

* * *

Говорят, если гложет тоска, измени
дом, страну, гардероб и прическу.
Я уже, и еще лик на облик страны
поменяла, и гвоздь на загвоздку.
В душный погреб души отнесла узелок
с небольшой, но весомой поклажей.
Кофе выпила, съела печенье, глоток
заглотила, наклюкалась даже.
Переставила мебель, сменила замки,
долго плешь проедала в народе,
отвечала на зовы судьбы и звонки,
всё напрасно – печаль не проходит.
Средства есть теперь всякие: от, как и для,
от разлуки с любимыми – тоже.
Я хочу быть с тобой до последнего дня
и потом, и потом, если можно.

* * *

They say if something's eating you, change your
house, your country, your wardrobe and hairstyle.
I've tried. I've even exchanged the country's features
for its profile and the nail for the snag.
I've carried into the airless cellars of the soul
my belongings in a small, but weighty, bag.
I drank some coffee, ate a biscuit, swallowed down
a gulp, even managed to get pissed,
changed the locks, moved the furniture around,
done my miserable stint in the crowd,
answered the calls of fate and the phone,
all to no avail – the pain won't go.
You can get anything now, potions for this and that
even for partings between lovers.
I want to be with you till the very last day.
and afterwards. Afterwards, if it's allowed.

[1995]

* * *

Кроме любви всё
покупается. Можно выкрасть,
захватить забодать милостыню просить.
Перейти в буддизм даже когда ты выкрест.
Перекроить мужика в бабу или же в травести.
Страшная может стать записной красоткой,
пожилая дама скостить лет пять,
негр - побелеть, черным стать гражданин Чукотки,
если поедет в Африку погулять.
Можно родить из пробирки, в мгновенье ока
в пыль превратить Нью-Йорк, полететь на Марс,
кроме любви
во всем воли больше, чем воли рока,
контртенором запевает бас.
Кроме любви и смерти и, впрочем, дара,
нам подвластно всё. Завоевать в бою
или пасть от вражеского удара,
но ни дать ни взять странный форпост *Лю
блю.*

* * *

Apart from love
everything can be bought. Try nicking,
grabbing, butting, try a begging plate.
Christian converts, try Buddhism.
Make a woman, or a travesty, out of a bloke.
Even the pig-ugly can become real babes.
Knock a good five years off a well-worn lady.
The black man can be white, an Eskimo, black
if he flies to Africa for fun.
Give birth out of a test-tube, in the blink of an eye
turn New York to dust, fly to Mars,
apart from love
in everything there's will enough to outwill fate,
a bass can lead in counter-tenor.
Apart from love, and death, and, oh yes, talent,
everything is ours to control. Win at Waterloo
or fall from enemy strike,
but there's no surrendering or taking the strange outpost: *Love
you.*

[1996]

* * *

Весь город озарен влеченьем,
все улицы - мои следы,
дома как теплые печенья
вбирают запахи среды.
К зеленым нервным окончаньям
кустов добавились цвета,
средь них бордовый - цвет печали
и всякая белиберда.
Вдруг город гаснет, вдруг, воочью
он, только что еще живой,
стоит, обуглившийся ночью,
днем - как покойник, восковой.
Смотрю в чужие окна, лица,
и со знакомого пути
сбиваюсь - может, в Альпах скрыться
иль как Суворов - перейти.

* * *

The whole town is lit by my desire.
All the streets are my traces.
The houses, like warm biscuits,
absorb the smells around them.
On the tips of green nerve endings
flowers picked from shrubs are placed,
amongst them claret – the colour of misery
and other senselessness.
Suddenly the town is darkened, suddenly,
I see it: alive not so long ago,
it looms, charred by night;
by day, a corpse, a waxwork.
I look through strangers' windows, faces
and stray from the familiar path –
maybe I'll hide out in the Alps,
or like Suvorov, march across.

[1991]

* * *

О любви я знаю так много и ничего почти,
вдыхая головокружительный, непривычный
воздух из рук, мне сжавших дыхательные пути
нежной змейкой и сказочной статью бычьей.
В гречневой каше, в киоске с картошкой ночном
столько любви, сколько по-детски мелом
писанных плюсов, сердечек формулы два в одном.
Засыпая во всех излучинах, излучаемых телом,
я не могу проспать ни одной версты,
нам разметившей вечность на километры,
где свой бешеный рэкет обрушит вдруг мир с высоты
в пику присланной мне колеснице попутного ветра.
Знаки сыпались градом и манною с двух полюсов,
я сажусь за алхимию, запах частиц не обманет,
страсть всегда убедительней, так что я в чаще усов
в кущу райскую ткнусь - и тихонько учусь мирозданью.

* * *

I know so much about love and almost nothing,
inhaling the dizzying, unfamiliar air
from the hands tightening around my windpipe,
with serpentine softness and the force of a fairytale bull.
In buckwheat porridge, in a chipstand at night,
there is as much love as there are children's
chalked pluses and hearts overlapping on walls.
I fall asleep in the spaces the body exposes.
But sleep through no more than a single verst
in this timelessness we have marked into miles
where one's fury-filled missile falls to explode over earth,
deterring the fair wind's chariot, coming my way.
Signs rained like hail or manna from both poles,
I try alchemy – the elements' scent won't deceive me.
Passion is always more urgent – in this thicket of feelers I crash
through the foliage of Paradise – and study creation with care.

[1999]

Весенний призыв

На современном русском языке
людей колбасит, плющит и ломает,
и мне в моем закукленном мирке
набор из грустных слов достался к маю:
тоска, протест, ориентиры врозь,
несбыточность, влекущая избыток
усердия к тому, что удалось
с одной или без всяческих попыток.

Набор пора убрать на антресоль,
достать оттуда летний – светлый, легкий,
который за зиму проела моль.
Почистить, подновить его и – плохо ль –
апрель – мажорный свет в конце зимы,
щетина на лице Земли пробилась
зеленая, и хлорофилл в умы
уж должен брызнуть был, чтоб пестик вылез,
тычинки, ореолы лепестков,
но в современном языке – не спелось
од радости, и мой набор таков,
что в нем звучит неутолимый мелос.

Весеннего призыва не смутясь,
слова косят от долга – от защиты
классического мира, что сейчас
исчезнет прямо как у Копперфилда.

Spring Conscription

In contemporary Russian
people 'get high', 'off their heads', they 'rave'.
But in my doll-like little world
a sad band of words has assembled by May:
dreariness; protest; pointers adrift;
and inaccessibility, which brings an excess
of zeal for things achieved
with little or even no attempt.

Time to put this band away for the season,
bring out the summer things – pale and light,
eaten through by the winter moths.
Dust them off, mend their cloth and – at last –
April – a major tone at the end of the winter.
Green stubble breaks out on the earth's
face, and chlorophyll should have sprayed
the mind, that a pistil might emerge
and stamens, the haloes of petals.
But in this contemporary language no Ode
to Joy resounds and my own band is such
that an unrelenting *melos* sounds.

Undeterred by spring conscription
the words dodge their duty: defence of
the classical world, fast disappearing
like one of Copperfield's magic tricks.

[2001]

31

* * *

Неужели я больше тебя никогда не увижу,
никогда не узнаю, здоров ли ты, даже жив ли?
От отметки привычной спускаюсь всё ниже, ниже,
ниже некуда, кажется, но бесконечны цифры.
Так и плачу в уютном своем, но пустынном доме,
ежевечерне вдовея, венчаясь снова.
У меня никого не осталось на свете кроме.
Я соврала, чтоб в дурной бесконечности вставить слово.
Неужели больше и голоса не услышу,
в рай не войду, в нирвану, лишь в супермаркет,
шляпку держа как съехавшую крышу,
с орангутаном кокетничая в зоопарке,
всё же надеясь на то, что однажды факсик
выплюнет мне утешительную депешу?
Я заплатила по самой высокой таксе,
жизнью, как здесь сказали бы нынче: кэшем.

* * *

Won't I ever see you again
or know if you're well, or even still alive?
I'm descending lower, lower, from my usual grade
till I must have reached the depths, but the numbers still dive.
So I sit and weep in the cosy desert of my home
every night a widow, and again a bride
with no one besides... I'm all alone
to slip a word in blank eternity I lied.
Won't I ever hear that voice
or find heaven or nirvana? Just the shop,
holding on to my hat, like it's my mind blowing loose,
with the orang-utan at the zoo I play the slut.
I'm still hoping that the fax one day
will spit out a consoling news flash.
I paid the very highest rate:
my life, round here they call it: *cash*.

[1996]

* * *

Как тигрица по клетке
в ожиданьи просвета,
то вино, то таблетки,
две зимы, снова лето
раскрывает ручонки
в хлорофилловой жажде,
и скребется в печенке,
и плывет всё отважней
по натянутым в струнку
острой тянущей болью
синим жилкам, и в бункер
рвется с бранного поля.
Плоть в заплатах медалей
за терпенье и веру,
в ней прострелены дали
как прыжки в атмосферу.

* * *

As a tigress stalks its cage
waiting for a ray of light,
could be wine, could be pills,
two winters, another summer
opens out its tiny hands
in thirst for chlorophyll,
and pecks at the liver
and sails ever bolder
along blue-blooded veins,
strung tight with nagging
pain and runs for the bunker
from the battlefield.
Flesh all patched with medals
for endurance and faith,
and shot through with distances
like leaps into space.

[1994]

Марафон

С какой неохотой я ставлю задачу
начать марафон одиночества.
Сижу за столом, пью Cointreau и не плачу,
мне ничего не хочется.

На предложенья заботливых граждан
развеять развлечь расслабиться,
я отвечаю честно и важно:
мне ничего не нравится.

Знаний полно: надо жить и работать,
не унывать от бешенства,
жизнь принимать как плохую погоду
и никогда не вешаться.

Не говорить "как мне плохо", напротив,
улыбаться: как здорово,
что города возвели на болоте,
что существует "Скорая".

Но неуклонно в ночном беспросветье
вперед выдается гласная:
"я" - быть в забеге одна на свете
не согласная.

Marathon

Reluctantly I give myself the task
of setting off on the lonely marathon.
I sit at the table, drink Cointreau, dry-eyed,
I don't want anything.

To caring citizens' offers
of taking me out of myself, entertaining, relaxing me,
I answer honestly and with gravity
I don't like anything.

I know it all: you've got to live and work
Not let madness get you down.
Take life as you would cold weather
and never hang yourself.

Never say, 'I feel bad'. On the contrary,
Smile: how wonderful it is
that towns were raised on marshes
and A&E exists.

But still in the night's dark desert
a vowel stands out in front –
'I' refuse to run like this –
quite alone in the world.

[1997]

37

Жемчужина

Жемчужина – бесплодие ракушки,
искусство вместо устрицы живой,
свет лампы вместо мякоти подушки,
свет-зеркальце как пес сторожевой.

Жемчужина – болезнь ракушки глупой,
не вовремя раскрывшей рот сказать:
«Я – будущая устрица из клуба
ложащихся на лед как на кровать».

Жемчужина из маленькой соринки
в глазу ракушки вес приобрела
как взгляд на жизнь, звезда с ночной картинки,
что освещает речку до утра.

Жемчужина – шедевр речного царства,
ракушку ищут демоны с земли,
чтобы продать ее талант как цацку.
Они и устриц, впрочем, извели.

Pearl

A pearl is the barrenness of a shell,
art in the place of live oyster,
lamplight in place of the soft pillow,
mirrored light like a dog on guard.

A pearl is the sore point of the silly shell
which didn't open its mouth in time to say,
'I am an oyster destined for that club
where one reclines on ice as if on a bed.'

The pearl, from a tiny mote of dust,
gained weight in the eye of the shell
like a glance at life, a star in a night picture
which illuminates the stream until dawn.

The pearl is the masterpiece of the river kingdom;
demons from the earth search for the shell
to sell its talent like a fairground charm
and destroy the oysters as they go.

[2001]

Замкнутый круг

Какой же ты замкнутый, круг!
Ни дырки в тебе, как в заборе,
ты даже не скреплен из дуг,
а просто бескраен, как море.
Тебя хоть в восьмерку свернуть -
дурной бесконечности знаком
и то не постичь твою суть.
Лишь звезды набив зодиаком
на голом твоем колесе,
возможно найтись по прописке,
проверив созвездия все.
Как все они могут быть близки,
но как далеки от меня,
кудрявые, лысые звезды!
Им даже не хватит огня
согреть меня осенью поздней,
им снега не хватит зимой,
весной - ручейков и тропинок,
в жару у них нет эскимо,
и врет гороскоп без запинок.
Есть формуле круга отпор:
движение пуще неволи -
бежать до тех сладостных пор,
что больше не чувствуешь боли.
Бежать от дождя, до угла,
без цели бежать, без оглядки.
а там где надежда легла -
там обруч, там мертвая хватка.

Vicious Circle

Circle, you're horribly round!
Fences have gaps, but not you.
You're not put together from curves,
you're limitless, just like the sea.
If I bent you into an eight,
barren infinity's sign,
I'd still not figure it out.
Only stars zodiac-formed
and carried on your bare wheel
are registered – they can be found,
if you check through the clusters of stars.
How close they might all become,
yet how far from me they all are,
those curly, bald-headed stars.
They don't even have enough warmth
to ward off late autumn's chill,
nor enough snow in the winter,
or streams and paths in the spring.
Their ice cream runs out in the heat,
and the horoscope lies through its teeth.
Try repulsing the circle like this:
movement out of captivity.
Run till the sweet realisation
that you can't feel the pain any more.
Run from the rain, to the corner,
without aim, without glancing behind you,
and there where once you found hope –
there's a hoop and you're back in its grip.

[1998]

* * *

Мне отключили горячую воду,
жидкость любви и словесный поток.
Мне бы пожаловаться народу,
но накинут платок на роток.
Так без живительной влаги и сохну,
с грязной посудой вдвоем.
Мхом порастаю, а может, и мохом,
может, и вовсе быльем.

* * *

They've turned off all the hot water,
my liquid of love, my stream of words.
I should complain to the people,
but a scarf's been thrown over my mouth.
Like this, without moisture of life, I'll dry out,
along with the unwashed dishes,
I'll gather moss, a stone unturned;
or perhaps be forgotten, lost in the grass.

[1995]

Нелюбит

Неопознанный, без мелодии слов, объятий,
как немое кино прострекочет секс.
Спрашивается в задаче: почему невозможно счастье,
неизбежна фрустрация, нуден стресс?
Вместо слияния вдруг пожнешь удушье,
поцелуй ноль градусов не пьянит,
ни хрена доверия: тут торчат не уши
а болезнь заразная - *нелюбит*.

Злобный вирус жизнь выживаньем морит,
неизвлекаем стал друг из друга кайф.
Хорошо вдвоем, но едет один на море
инфицированный - у всех свой нрав,
если б не эпидемия нестыковок,
запаршивели овцы, с них шерсти на память клок.
Трудно вымолвить, будь ты хитер и ловок:
"Я живу хорошо" - я беру эту фразу в долг.

Viral infection: Lovelessness

Unidentified, without melody of words, embraces,
sex flickers past like a silent film.
I set myself a question: why is happiness beyond hope,
frustration inevitable, why is stress so dull?
No bodily amalgamation, but sudden asphyxiation;
a nought percent kiss hardly goes to the head,
there's fuck-all trust: it's not the ears sticking out
but the contagious disease of Lovelessness.

This bug destroys life by grimly hanging on.
Ecstasy is no longer caught from another.
It's good together, then one goes away
infected, alone – we're none of us the same.
If only it hadn't been for the epidemic of mismatches,
the flocks of black sheep, bad apples in batches.
It's hard to proclaim, as if adept, a dab hand,
'I have a nice life'. I loan this phrase from the bank.

[1999]

* * *

Могла быть счастлива как бобик,
с хозяином на поводке,
могла протявкать: бесподобен
мир и подстилка в закутке.
Но в жизни так не получилось
и, говоря уж всё как есть,
я как Маруся – отравилась,
девичью запятнала честь.
С тех пор я стала ядовита
и мудрой злобности полна.
Я проклинаю тот напиток,
и пью до дна.

* * *

I could have been as happy as a dog
with my master on a leash,
I could have yapped: all's right with the world –
my bed is under the chimneypiece.
But it didn't happen to me like that –
I'll tell it as it really was,
like Marusya, I drank the poison,
my girlish reputation lost.
From then on I was poisonous
and full of wise gall.
I curse that very same drink
and drink it all.

[1995]

Ночь перед рождеством

Под Рождество пространство онемело,
задув мою свечу у изголовья.
Кто выбирает каменную стену,
а кто, как я - крючок для рыбной ловли.

Я в черную дыру свалилась с нашей
ухоженной, сияющей планеты,
тут пусто, но в глазах привычно пляшет
предмет, вернее, видимость предмета.

Кровать - явленье высшего порядка,
что жизнь дает и отбирает разом,
бывая дном, бывая сочной грядкой.
Вот спряталась, накрывшись медным тазом.

Под Рождество гадают и желают,
но в черной дырке всей обратной мощью
песнь ангелов звучит охрипшим лаем.
Здесь край - где лишь проклятья и возможны.

Christmas Eve

On the night before Christmas space was numbed
once it had blown out my bedside candle.
Some of us choose a wall of stone,
some, like me, a hook in the fishing tackle.

I fell from our well-tended, shining
Planet down into a black hole.
It was empty, but an object dances as usual
in my eyes, or perhaps the semblance is all.

Bed is a phenomenon of that highest order
whereby life gives and at once takes back.
It can be day, it can be a well-stocked border –
then it hides itself away, gone, and that's that.

On Christmas Eve wishes and predictions are made,
but in the black hole with all power reversed
the songs of the angels sound like hoarse howls.
This is the land where only curses are heard.

[1997]

49

* * *

Как может жизнь на столь протяжный срок
из сносной стать совсем невыносимой,
когда - ну всё не то, товарищ Бог,
погода, экология, мужчины.
И даже лай собак - не тех собак,
ласкавших слух бетховенно, шопенно,
трава в себя влекла любовный акт,
но то ж была трава - не листья сенны!
Мой Бог, ты как не мой, ты за хазар
что ль задним стал числом, а не за наших,
которым - отвечаю за базар -
чем дальше в лес, тем волки воют чаще.

* * *

How can life, for such a prolonged period,
go from being bearable to being a total bane,
when – it's not like it should be, Comrade God,
the weather, the environment, the men.
Even the dogs' barking – its not those dogs
who caressed the ear so beethoveny, chopinish,
the grass drew into itself the act of love,
but that was real grass – not these hay wisps!
My Lord, its like you're not mine, like you've given your word
retrospectively to the Southern tribes, thrown in the towel
with us, for whom, and, I mean this, Lord,
the further we go in the forest, the more the wolves howl.

[1997]

* * *

Прощай, прощай, поэзия,
российский двор, порожек,
прощайте все претензии
на то что Бог поможет.

Душа - сплошная ссадина,
и в бездне унижений
свело ей мускул пряденый.
Прощай же, пораженье!

Прощай, домашний оберег,
любовь, счастливый полюс,
я недопела в опере,
я потеряла голос.

Как с чучелом обвенчана,
из миски пью до донышка,
мне чудилось быть женщиной
да завести ребеночка.

В Берлине стенка рухнула,
всех перетасовала,
смела, убила, стукнула.
Я вышла в тень провала.

Прощанье ритуальное -
прощанье понарошке:
"прощай" - итог, испарина,
заклятье черной кошки.

* * *

Farewell, farewell to poetry,
a Russian yard, a doorstep,
Farewell to all illusion
That we might get God's help.

The soul is all abrasion
and in this, abasement's pit,
the spinning muscle cramps.
Farewell to you, defeat!

Farewell to the shelter of a home,
to love, the happy side of life,
I didn't sing the opera through
I lost my voice.

Like marrying a scarecrow,
I drink deep from the bowl,
I dreamed I was a woman, she
brought a child into the world.

In Berlin the wall collapsed
and shook us all about,
it consumed and killed and spied upon.
In its shadow I walked out.

A ritual farewell-taking –
a farewell with intention:
'goodbye' – tot up, evaporate,
a black cat's incantation.

[1994]

Грипп

Добрые люди пришли,
накормили меня, больную,
но не поцеловали,
будто я тоже вирус.

Саша принес мне фрукты,
Андрей - можжевеловой водки,
Коля - платков носовых,
папа - вареной свеклы,
Галя - салат "Столичный",
Влад - расфасованный сыр.

Внутри себя чувствую конкурс:
кто больше всех пожалел
гриппом сраженное тело?

Flu

All the nice people came round
to feed me, sick as I was,
but they gave me no kisses
like I was a virus myself.

Sasha brought me some fruit,
Andrei some juniper vodka,
Kolya brought packets of hankies,
my Dad brought boiled red beet.
Galya brought mayonnaise salad,
Vlad brought spreadable cheese.

Inside I sense competition:
who, of all, felt most compassion
for this body, racked by the flu?

[1999]

* * *

Если надеть предмет по имени шуба,
будет даже зима поганая люба.
Выйдя в созвездье плюсов, минуя вычет,
не моргнув, когда минусы кличут, кличут,
мы тепло генерируем - так галактики
начинают сближаться. (В научной практике
все разбегаются в ужасе, прочь от взрыва,
от космической стужи, ее наплыва).
Сочетаться теплом веселей, чем браком:
нету полости, где б заводиться шлакам,
ни наследства Адама - заболеванья
"хочешь счастья, а получаешь знанья".

* * *

If you put on that thing called a fur coat
even the filthiest winter will be sweet.
Going out into a constellation of pluses, avoiding the drop,
not turning a hair at minuses' constant tug,
we generate heat – that's how the galaxies
come closer. (In scientific theory
everything flees in horror from the big bang,
from cosmic frost with its icy fingers.)
Creating heat is more fun than marriage contracting:
no cavities for the rubbish to collect in.
Nor Adam's legacy – that indisposition:
'You wanted happiness, but you'll get wisdom.'

[1999]

* * *

Что осталось от козлика? Рожки,
простые рога.
Ножек совсем не осталось,
длинных и стройных.
Козлик пустился в бега,
и в копытце нога -
всё что полиция может сказать
о приметах забойных.
Люди, сыщите мне козлика,
тушку и шерсть,
гладить, чесать ее буду,
и время замерив,
буду смотреть, как оно истекает из зверя,
 нечеловеческий мне сообщая замес.

* * *

What's left of the goat? Its horns,
just its horns.
Nothing left of its legs,
long and slender.
The goat took to its heels
and the cloven-hoofed legs
are all that the police can reveal
of the livestock's distinguishing marks.
Good people, track down the goat,
its carcass, its hair,
I'll stroke it and scratch it,
and when time has stood still,
I'll watch to see how it drains from the beast
imparting to me the non-human mix.

[1995]

* * *

Меня убивает бессилье
пчелы, что осталась без улья,
что тьма сколдовалась из сини
и то что меня обманули.

Цветов навидавшись до ряби,
пыльцою набита как пылью -
ее б претворить по-приапьи.
Как русский уча: "рыбы плыли",
я всё повторяю: ее бы
в секрецию света, в янтарный
густеющий всплеск, без микроба,
без пены, без дыма, без раны.

Ее бы в медок на розетке
на дачной террасе за чаем,
дед с бабушкой: "На тебе, детка",
а я: "не хочу", - отвечаю.
И я не хочу и не буду,
мой выбор пока беспределен,
заставы, побеги, запруды,
душа еще как бы не в теле.

И вот наступает мгновенье,
где всё окончательно, ясно,
нет проб и ошибок, сомнений,
всё так, а не эдак, и баста.

* * *

The helplessness of a bee left without
a hive, the dark magicking itself out of deep blue,
and how I was deceived: these things kill me.

Dazzled by the endless flowers,
stuffed with pollen and dust –
the bee should transformed by Priapus.
Like a tongue twister 'swim swan swam'
I repeat again: the bee should go
into the secretion of light, the amber
clotting splash, germ-free,
foam-free, smoke-free, wound-free.

It should be in the dish of honey
on the dacha terrace at tea-time,
Grandma, Grandpa saying, 'Have some, child'
and me answering, 'No. Don't want it.'
And so I don't and so I won't,
my choice is still limitless,
gates, flight, ponds of standing water,
it's as if the soul hasn't yet put on flesh.
Then all at once comes a moment
When everything is certain and clear,
no more trials, mistakes or doubts:
it's this way, not that: and that's it.

[1994]

* * *

Как мечта не усохнет, не сморщится, маясь?
Месяцами за ней наблюдаю и удивляюсь:
ведь она не какая-то там маракуйя,
а глава из жизни, но не могу я
делать вид, что за ней еще главы, главы.
Кто за истину видимость примет - правы.
В окруженьи количеств урчу как котик,
с ними жгу электричество, не наркотик,
но во времени плюсквамперфект дышу
и курю - повторяю, не анашу -
с тем кого уж давно нет рядом,
и сквозь дым его отмечаю взглядом.

* * *

How is it the dream doesn't dry up, crinkle in suffering?
I've been watching it for months now and wondering.
After all, its hardly an exotic plant,
just a chapter from life, yet I can't
pretend that after it there'll be chapters indefinitely.
They are right, the ones who take appearance for reality.
In the company of numbers I growl like a cat.
I burn electricity with them, and not hash,
but when I think of the past, I breathe
and smoke – not a joint, I repeat –
with the one who hasn't been around in an age,
and through the smoke I catch him in my gaze.

[1999]

* * *

Что воешь, трубка, как сирена,
не шепчешь мне на ушко сказок?
Выходит, что и вечность бренна:
сошла с ума, ушла на базу.
А я в нее вложила годы
дизайнерства и модельерства,
искала новые подходы,
писала "хуй" на занавеске.
Я вечность прождала в подъезде,
в истерзновеньи телефонном,
она всегда была на месте,
своем заведомом, посконном.
И вот теперь прошло и это,
и свято место пусто, мглисто,
вся вечность - времени примета,
и hasta, стало быть, la vista.

* * *

Receiver, why wail like a siren?
Whisper a story in my ear?
Seems like even eternity passes:
goes mad, or simply out to tea.
I invested years in it,
years of couture and design,
searched for new approaches,
wrote *fuck* on the window-blind.
I waited out eternity in the entrance hall –
tormented by the telephone.
It was always there at hand,
known by all, ages old.
And now all that has passed as well.
It's little corner – empty, dim.
All eternity only a mark of time,
and *la vista*, *hasta*, it would seem.

[1995]

* * *

Как не хватает этого, а чего - не знаю,
когда жажда неиссякаема, хоть и удовлетворима,
когда ужин нельзя завершить чашкой кофе иль кружкой чаю
в силу взаимогравитации нестерпимой.
Все равно остаются с нелюбимыми и нелюбящими,
с ними всегда оказывается сподручнее.
Так что притяженье Земли преодолимо в будущем,
но куда отслаивается всё тактильное, поцелуйчатое?
Куда делись нескончаемые беседы? Неразличимость,
где кончается *я* и начинается *ты*? Жизнь прогнулась,
стала похожа на функцию синус,
утомительную немоту, сутулость.
Планка осела, над нею как над могилкой
я сижу на корточках и не могу смириться.
Как таинствен был мир в золотых прожилках,
как теперь насильно закрыта моя граница.

* * *

I'm missing something. What it is I don't know,
when thirst is unquenchable, yet may be satisfied;
when dinner won't end after tea and coffee's served
and all because of this terrible mutual gravity.
It's all the same to the unloved and unloving,
with them things are always far more comfortable.
So perhaps, one day, we will overcome Earth's pull.
But where is the tactile, the kiss-scaled shaved off to?
Where did the unending conversations go? The individable,
where *I* end and *you* begin? Life has caved in,
has started to resemble a sine-wave graph,
a wearying numbness, a hunched back.
The ground beneath my feet has subsided and upon it,
as if on a gravestone, I squat and cannot reconcile
this: how mysterious it was, the golden-veined globe
and now how my border has been forcibly closed.

[1999]

Рунет

Больше нет страны РФ на свете,
нет России - есть страна Рунет.
АБВ нет, аза, буки, веди,
Костромы с Камчаткой тоже нет.
www – новопрестольный город,
сайты поселений всех мастей:
есть понаселенней, где за ворот
килобайт бежит, набрав вестей,
есть понебоскребистей – порталы,
в баннеров цветастых витражах,
есть покомпроматистей, как скалы,
там где горцы бьются на ножах.
А бывают целые поселки
трехэтажных сайтов без жильцов,
пляжи, где как огурцы в засолке,
загорают все, в конце концов.
В чаты заползает человечек,
ищет непрерывности пути.
Хакер-истребитель бомбы мечет,
в письмах шлет их, свесившись с сети.
Так живет Рунет, несутся линки,
в паутине не осталось дыр,
мышки так и щелкают ботинком,
уплетая свой бесплатный сыр.
Власть географическая пала,
мы переселились по хостам,
где, средь исторического бала
мир переместился на экран,
слег как сыч в коробку с монитором,
мы играем с ним по одному,
так отпало общество, в котором
все играли в пробки и в войну.

Ru.net

The Russian Federation has ceased to exist,
Russia is no more – only Ru.net is left.
No more ABC, *aza*, *buki*, *vedi*,
neither Kostroma or Kamchatka survives.
WWW is the new reigning city,
'sites' are the settlements for all the trades:
there are those more established, where beyond the gate
a kilobyte circulates, bursting with news,
there are the sky-scraped ones, the portals
covered in banners' garish stained-glass light,
there are those more extreme, like the cliffs
where mountain people fight it out with knives
and there are whole settlements, too,
uninhabited sites on three floors,
beaches, where like sardines in a tin,
everyone gets a tan by the end of the day.
A little person squeezes into a chatroom
searching for the continuation of a path.
A hacker-hitman flings his bombs,
sends them in letters, hanging from the net.
And this is Ru.net: lines rushing madly,
no holes left in the spider's web.
The mice there clicking with their shoes
and squirreling away the gratis cheese.
Geographical might has fallen,
we have resettled along the lines of hosts,
where, at the height of a historical ball
the world was re-sited onto a screen
and glumly rests itself in a monitor-box.
We play with it, one by one, and how
society falls away – the same society
in which we played the fool and played at war.

[2001]

ru.net: a common Russian website address.

Исток Волги

Две опаленных птички, лебедь чокнутый
и чахлый ворон, подлетели в танце
к истоку Волги - в караул почетный.
Черёд легендам набело писаться.
Истории российской черновик
сгорел, чтоб выплыл чистый лист, родник,
прозрачный свиток с глиняной печаткой,
земля остановилась здесь на миг.
В пейзажеобразующем волненьи
вдруг зелень золоченую пургой
хлестнет из тучи - жизнь пошла рекой
без права на помарки: взяв теченье,
должна вода до моря доползти,
намыв нам берегов в пересеченьи
и птицам чистя перья по пути.

The Source of the Volga

Two singed birds: a rabid swan
and a runt of a raven, flew down in a dance
to the source of the Volga, to mount guard of honour.
It's time to write out the legends in fair.
The rough copy of Russian history
was burnt so a clean sheet might float free, a spring,
a transparent page with a clay stamp upon it,
the world stopped here momentarily.
In agitation to form the land
the gilded green was lashed
by a blizzard from a cloud – life gushed forward as a river
with no right to correction: once it takes direction
water must crawl as far as the sea,
washing our banks as it crosses the land,
cleaning the birds' feathers on its way.

[1999]

Грани

Пленка-ночь засвечена, весь день я
сторожу границу тонких граней.
Где в защиту вкралось нападенье?
Как тротилом стал лукум в Коране?

Шли с ножом, а может, пошутили.
Я кулак держу – обороняюсь.
Разные у нас, однако, стили.
Может победить и нож, и палец.

Свет стал витражом на черной пленке,
подписал ее, прихорошился
в зеркале, чувствительном настолько,
что о новый свет разбился, смылся,

стал бельмом, и пленка стала лысой,
черная дыра как страж хранила
россыпь глаз, прикрас, смешных капризов.
Луч звезды нас стер, сварил на мыло.

Тьма и свет, как в танце, поменялись
позами, друг друга ослепили.
Нож отбросил мой когтистый палец,
перешедший грань лежит в эндшпиле.

Может, я ответом стерла просто
нож как острый знак, как восклицанье,
и за ним стоявший - стал апостол,
я же превратилась в отрицанье.

В черную дыру свалились оба.
Нас хранить бессрочно обещайте,
только пусть мой луч, мой Бог, мой опыт
Подождет проявки и печати.

Edges / Lines

Film/night is exposed, all day I
guard the border of fine lines.
Where did attack creep into defence;
the Koran's sweetmeats become explosives?

They came with blades, could have been feigning.
I make a fist – to arm myself.
Still, we all have our own ways of being:
both a knife and a finger may bring defeat.

The light was stained glass on the black film,
it signed the film, adjusted its face
in the mirror, so very sensitive
that it broke on the new world, slipped away,

became a cataract, and the film was blank,
the black hole guards like a sentry post
that sprinkling of eyes, ornament, caprices.
The starlight erased us, boiled us down to soap.

Dark and light switched poses as if
dancing, they blinded one another.
My clawed hand throws away the knife,
the crossed line lies in the endgame.

Or perhaps with my answer I erased the knife
like a sharp-edged sign, an exclamation,
and what was behind became an apostle,
and I in turn became a denial.

Both plunged deep into a black hole.
Promise to keep us for all time,
only let my light, my God, my life
wait for developing, fixing and printing.

[2002]

73

* * *

Чтоб не было видно, ночами кончается лето,
уходит земля из-под ног, покрываясь асфальтом,
и выцветшей тряпкой купальник валяется, бедный,
что было под ним - еле живо под длинным халатом.

Листва стала грубой, слова и ботинки под дождик.
И нежность, возможно, уже никогда не проснется,
она так же смертна как вот, расфырчавшийся ёжик,
нашедший подругу в траве с дураком длинноносым.

Ах лето, с собой уносящее столики с улиц,
из теплых садов уводящее голые спины,
попала под дождь - а как будто попала под пули,
чего-то сказали - а будто бы просто избили.

* * *

Summer ends at night, so as not to be seen,
the ground beneath our feet disappears beneath asphalt.
And a faded scrap of a swimsuit lies around, poor thing,
what was in it, barely alive under a long housecoat.

The leaves are now rough, like words and shoes in the rain.
And tenderness, it is possible, may now never wake up.
It's as mortal as that hedgehog, all puffed and pained,
who found his girl in the grass with some long nosed chap.

O Summer, carrying off the café tables from the streets,
leading bare backs out of the warm parks,
I was caught in the rain and it felt like bullets –
they spoke to me, it felt like they'd beaten me up.

[1991]

* * *

Каких бы дождь не выкапал слезинок,
чужому слуху он - стеклянный бисер,
я вижу тучу черную, ботинок
промокший, блеск простудный на карнизе.

Я собственного голоса не слышу,
поскольку не свершилось диалога,
и я стучу компьютеру как мышка
куриной лапой телеграмму, долго
стучу шепча, чтобы согрелся на ночь
кусочек тишины под одеялом,
мне колыбельный храп соседский Палыч
споет, под звуки дрели утром встану.

Когда дуэт фальшивит, вянут уши,
я глазки долу опустив, не вижу,
что расцветают яблони и груши
а может, листья падают на крыши.

* * *

However many tears the rain may let drop
to another's ear it's a glass bead.
I see a black cloud, a shoe
wet through, the feverish glint on the cornice.

I don't hear my own voice
since no dialogue has taken place,
and I tap the computer like a mouse,
illegible scribblings like a bird's, for a long
long while I tap, whispering, to warm through
a corner of silence beneath the blanket at night.
A neighbour's snored lullaby sings me to sleep,
I wake up in the morning to the sound of a drill.

When there's a wrong note in the duet, offending the ear
I drop my eyes and don't see
how they blossom, the apple and pear trees
and maybe leaves are falling on the roofs.

[1999]

* * *

Диктатура ли, демократия,
хоть по выбору, хоть насильно -
результат все равно отрицательный,
если речь идет о России.

Если жизнь сикось-накось-выкуси,
набекрень, на бровях, на спуске,
всё погибло и цикл зациклился -
значит, ты - настоящий русский.

Здесь фонтан вместо чаш терпения,
нам последнюю каплю - вычли.
В точке взлета, паденья, кипения -
очи козочьи, шеи бычьи.

* * *

Dictatorship, democracy,
voted in or seized the nation,
the result is still a mockery
where Russia rules the conversation.

If life's all half-arsed, get arsed,
pear-shaped, half-baked, gone to pot,
everything lost, the wheel spinning fast –
you are a Russian, like as not.

We've a fountain, not a cup, of patience,
but they've taken back the dregs.
At the point of incidence, boiling, take-off,
you'll find goats' eyes and bulls' necks.

[1998]

Кровать

С сопутствующим учащеньем пульса
весь мир мастрячит бомбы, как в кино.
День, выйдя в ночь, за горизонт загнулся,
с утра, во сне, мне это все равно.
Но грянул взрыв, и вся архитектура
покрылась слоем порчи и говна.
Мы строили свой град, свою натуру
надстраивали вверх: видна стена,
которой ум и разум ограждали
от полчищ непонятной саранчи,
а может, мы себе срезали дали:
боялись всевозможностей в ночи.
Мы постепенно шли, от камня к камню,
в воздвиженьи соборов и дворцов,
с холма в долину двигались, руками
ощупывая почву праотцов.
Мы помыслы свои запечатляли,
себя пред небом славя: мол, растем,
творим и в алфавите, и в металле,
мы – зодчие, еще немного шьем.
И вдруг какой-то леший колченогий
нас стал стыдить, смеялся нам в лицо:
вы прах земли, вы стали в позу, йоги,
на цыпочки, придумав им крыльцо.
Мы посмотрели на себя критично
и выпили по маленькой вина,
иные, устыдившись, град тепличный
покрыли слоем порчи и говна,
другие в медитации замкнулись,
а кто пошел добро распродавать.
Я просыпаюсь, вижу – нету улиц,
есть чуть помятый мир – моя кровать.

Bed

To the accompaniment of a racing pulse
the whole world makes bombs, like in the films.
Day gives way to night and crouches behind the horizon,
I couldn't care less in the morning, in my dreams.
But, just at that very moment, they covered
the architecture in a layer of dust and shit.
We build our town, we overbuilt it
with our nature: the walls are clear
that we built around our reason
to shield it from strange plagues of locusts
and maybe we cut off our distant prospects,
fearing at night all manner of things.
We moved continuously from stone to stone
erecting cathedrals and palaces,
we came down from hill to valley, hands
groping for our ancestors' land.
We imprinted it with our intentions,
gave glory to ourselves before the heavens: see, we grow
we create in letters and in metal,
we're architects, we've not much left to create.
When suddenly some bandy-legged sprite
shamed us, laughing in our face:
'You're the earth's remains – but you assume the pose,
yogi on tiptoes, you even thought up plinths for your toes.'
We looked critically at ourselves,
drank just a little drop of wine,
others, ashamed, covered the town of glass
in a layer of dust and shit.
Others wrapped themselves in meditation,
and some went off to sell their goods.
I wake up, look round – the streets are gone,
there is only the slightly crumpled world of bed.

[2001]

* * *

Тишина похожа на темноту, наркоз,
замкнутое пространство.
Я забыла, как жить в мороз,
с его снежной массой.
Зазеркален блеск амальгамы чувств
сквозь метель смятенья.
И фонтан замерз, и загашник пуст,
и сдалось растенье.

* * *

Silence is like the dark, a drug,
a sealed space.
I have forgotten how to live in the cold
with its snowy wastes.
The alloy of feelings has a looking-glass gleam
through the blizzard bewildered.
The fountain is frozen, the hiding place empty,
the plant has surrendered.

[1999]

Очки

Блин горелый, ядреная вошка,
я надела очки, мне всё видно,
мне светло в них, и чайная ложка
с медом лезет мне в рот, и копытом
лошадь бьет под окном - знак дороги,
знак отмены терзания в пробках,
и вообще - я полна аналогий,
я в очках перестала быть робкой.

Я взираю с беспечным сарказмом
на подвал, где меня истязали
порционно пускаемым газом -
это все было в греческом зале,
я стояла обломком богини,
ослепленной еще в Возрожденье,
но в техническом веке, отныне
мне вернулось холодное зренье.

Я как прежде хотела бы верить,
что божественный трепет колышет
наши неуглядимые перья,
но очки мне сказали, что ниши
занимают согласно билетам.
Свет кончается, гаснет, я в ложах
всех раздетыми вижу, как летом,
вижу я и себя - толстокожей.

Ясный перец, братишки сестренки,
мы вступили в опасные связи,
есть в терзаньях души две коронки:
страсть слепая и видимость трассы.

Glasses

Well I never. Holy shit.
I've put on glasses, I can see.
Everything in them is bright, the honeyed
teaspoon slips into my mouth, hooves
sound under the window: a sign of the road,
a sign of an end to traffic hell,
and generally – I am full of comparisons
and in glasses I've stopped being shy.

I regard with footloose sarcasm
the basement where they tortured me
with released gas in little bursts –
that was all in the Greek Room,
I stood there like a goddess fragment,
blinded back in the Renaissance,
but in the techno-age, henceforth
my sight is returned, clear and cold.

As before, I'd like to think
that a divine shiver moves
our imperceptible plumes
but my glasses tell me that the niches
are occupied by ticket holders.
The light dies, goes out and in the stalls
I see them undressed, as if sunbathing
I see myself, my thicker skin.

Bleeding obvious, brothers, sisters,
we've entered in on dangerous liaisons.
Two high points in the soul's torment:
blind passion, visibility ahead.

[1999]

* * *

Каждый прожитый день - это плюс или минус,
больше пыли нанес или мусора вынес?
Приголубит судьба, а из голубя - гриф,
вдруг как цапнет когтями и бросит на риф.
Так невроз укусил меня в детскую пятку,
ахиллесовым сделав во мне по порядку
все от органов доброго сна до желез,
выделяющих сладость, и нервы в вопрос
изогнулись: зачем им обрезали крылья,
нашим ангелам, тем, что над миром парили,
над землею безвидной, над бездной и тьмой
показав нам ее претворенье в лесной
и озерный, щебечущий, пахнущий остров
на свету золотой, в приближении - пестрый?
Я-то думала: так оно будет всегда,
чудо-люди, как чудо - огонь и вода,
но возникли шумы, и помехи, и сбой,
нас же предупредили: следи за собой.
Почему стало скучно, и страшно, и "через
не хочу" или "ешь что дают" - натерпелись
жить не так как задумано, всё - перегрузка,
зло берет и желание нового пуска.

* * *

Is every passed day a plus or a minus?
Does it layer with dust, or take out the crap?
Fate dove-like caresses – then dove turns griffin,
takes a sharp clawing hold, throws its prey on a reef.
So neurosis once bit me on my childish heel
making everything in me Achillean in turn
from the organs of sound sleep to the glands
releasing sweetness. My nerves curled into
a question: why did they clip the wings
of our angels, the ones who soared above the world,
above the invisible earth, the abyss and the darkness,
showing us its transformation into the forested
laked, the twittering, scented isle,
shining gold in the light and close up brightly coloured?
So there was I thinking it would always be like that:
miracle-people, like the miracles of water and fire,
but there was trouble, and problems and battles arose –
'cause they did warn us to 'look after ourselves'.
And then it was boring and horrible and 'I told you
so' or 'eat what you're given' – and we patiently
learned to live, but not as we'd dreamed, the whole lot
a burden: all anger inside and the desire for a new start.

[1999]

* * *

Если всё в прошлом, что остается делать,
как наряжаться в сари воспоминаний,
делить на отрезы безразмерную ткань тела
с зарубками по годкам - Паркиными коготками.
(Но теперь я думаю о мясистом ухвате Рока:
счет игры - в пользу мужского пола,
бледная трепонема, трихомонада и палка Коха!
"Сам дурак" - лихорадочный плач Эбола.)
Прошлое кончилось седьмого июля
тясяча девятьсот девяносто шестого года:
раскаленная лава внезапно застыла в пулю.
Жизнь после смерти рассказывать неохота.
До - оттенки, тенёта, теньки и тенты,
до - светлячки, светёлки, светила, свитки,
до - поражались фригидные, импотенты,
что бывает в жизни вот так - в избытке.
Ангел-хранитель, кажется мне, растерян,
от кого охранять клиента, что в прошлогодних
кринолинах зарылся глухой тетерей?
Что ни пой - все мотивы ему не годны.

* * *

If all is past and gone, what remains to be done
but clothe oneself in the sari of memories,
cut the body's one-size fabric into dress lengths
With notches for the years – the claw marks of the Parcae.
(But now I'm thinking of Fate's meaty grasp:
the game score stands in favour of the men,
the pale bacteria of the sexually transmitted,
the coccus, Ebola's feverish accusing cry.)
The past came to an end on the seventh of July
in the year of ninety six when, without warning
red hot lava set hard into a bullet
and life after death isn't worth the telling.
Before there were shades, shacks, shadows, shafts,
before there were fireflies, fiery stars, files, fire,
before the frigid and impotent were amazed
that life could be like that – a real horn of plenty.
The guardian angel is bewildered, or so it seems to me
from whom should he guard the client, head buried
in past years' crinolines, as deaf as deaf can be?
Whatever you sing, he won't enjoy the melody.

[1997]

* * *

Мне хочется снять с себя панцирь, доспехи
наросших в душе тупиков, компромиссов,
бывает, возрадуюсь: вот и успехи
терпенья, тут фейсом об тейбл, я кисну,
скулю, увядаю и делаюсь центром,
раз нет половинки, с которой поделишь
прижизненный ужас, и страх перед смертью,
и счастье - единственный, в сущности, фетиш.
Я целое, если целуюсь, и вертел
с нанизанным мясом, предавшийся думам,
когда я сама на бессмысленном свете
сражаюсь то с бурей, то с диким самумом.

* * *

I'd like to free myself from the chainmail, the armour
of dead ends and compromises, encrusting my soul.
There are times when I'm up – when I'm succeeding
in being patient. Then my face is back, pressed on the table.
I grow sour, I whimper, I make myself the centre
as there's no other half with whom one might share
the horrors in life and the fear before death,
and happiness, the single and only real fetish.
I'm complete when I kiss, otherwise a spit
threaded with meat and given to thought,
when I fight in this meaningless world by myself
sometimes with a tempest, sometimes a simoom.

[1999]

* * *

Хочется – сбудется, только позднее, чем надо.
Между Землей и Мечтой – световые года.
Нынче за ужином капельки яда
всё выступали на нёбе и меркла еда.
Звуки во тьме очевидней, и чавканье тоже.
Грузный партнер засыпает как сом.
Вот и еще один день не с тобой – героически прожит,
так что хоть волосы дыбом, да грудь колесом.
Всё посбывалось, лишь ты остаешься не сбытым
чудом на рынке Господнем. Заказ устарел:
хоть ты и кальцием стал бы, седым трилобитом,
жизнь без тебя всё равно – беспросветный пробел.
Ты нас не знаешь, российских бестрепетных ланей,
наше терпение терпче французских духов,
наша любовь – бесконечней любых расстояний,
нам до Мечты – как до самых простых Васюков.

* * *

If you want enough you get, but later than you needed.
The Earth and the Dream are light years apart.
Today at dinner, tiny drops of poison
kept rising to the palate, and the meal faded to dark.
In darkness, sounds are clearer – the slurping of food.
My overloaded partner sinks to sleep, doesn't float.
Yet another day without you, survived like a hero,
my hair may stand on end, but my hero's chest is out.
Everything has come true, you alone remain a promised
miracle at God's Fair. I ordered long ago:
you may be calcium now, a greying fossil-shell
yet life without you is a lightless, hopeless hole.
You don't know us, we're bold Russian Bambis,
our patience has more pungence than any French perfume,
our love is more infinite than any single distance,
from us to the Dream is a step across the room.

[1995]

Женщина

Я надеваю помаду и тушь,
крем, разноцветные пряжи и ткани.
Тысячи глаз превращаются в сканер,
видя в огне меня, ставя под душ,
в сад усадив меня в кресле плетеном,
свет процедив через крон кружева:
кожа – экран, принимающий сонм
звезд на веснушчатом небе. Слова
шерсткой меня покрывают, сгущаясь
нимбом над круглой болванкой лица.
Я улыбаюсь в ответ и смущаюсь.
Или сражаюсь, как зверь, до конца.

Woman

I put on lipstick, mascara,
cream, different coloured yarns and threads.
Thousands of eyes become a scanner
which sees me in the fire, places me under a shower
or leaves me seated in a wicker chair in the garden,
filtering the light through the lace of branches:
the skin is a screen, it takes on the throng
of stars in the freckled sky. Words
cover me in their wool, it fluffs out
like a halo around the pointless roundness of my face.
I smile in answer, and feel uneasy.
Or I fight like a beast to the very end.

[2002]

* * *

Почему же вы все меня бросили, папа и мама,
почему вы меня, дед и бабушка, не защитите!
Я устала от лжи, что вокруг меня вьется как дама
пик на каждом балу, под невиданным раньше покрытьем.
Я устала от боли, от трудностей, преодоленья
всех пинков и плевков в суть мне данного слабого пола.
Я выносливей ишака, но до дрожи в коленях
не умею снести стрел Амура кривого укола.
И опять уходя - от обиды, с гноящейся ранкой,
бормочу, не упрек, не молитву, а как в детском саде:
что ж вы бросили, папа и мама, меня как подранка,
где ж вы, бабушка, дед, чтоб меня по головке погладить!

* * *

Why have you both left me, Dad, Mum?
Why don't you defend me, Grandad, Nan?
I'm tired of the lies winding around me like the Queen
of Spades at every ball, undercover and invisible until now.
I'm tired of the pain, hardship, overcoming
all the kicks and spits at the heart of my given weaker sex.
I'm more patient than a donkey, but down to knees trembling
I don't know how to bear the jab of Cupid's bent shaft.
And once more departing from the hurt, with festering wound
I mutter like at nursery, no reproach, nor a prayer:
Why have you dropped me, Mum and Dad, like wounded game,
where are you, Nanny, Grandad, to stroke me on the hair?

[1997]

SELECTED PROSE

A Recent History of Moscow

I don't altogether understand what Russia is. It is too vast, too multilingual, too multicultural. I haven't even travelled over a fifth of its territory, and that's not even taking into account its constantly changing geographical and political outlines. So my homeland is Moscow and my people are the Muscovites, those born in Moscow or those that settled in Moscow, wherever they originally came from: deep in the Russian provinces, other countries, or from the former Soviet republics. There is one special circumstance, which links me with Moscow. We are the same age. Of course I don't mean I was born in 1147, but the life of Moscow is like the history of a race, consisting of the birth, flourishing and death of each generation. An individual's life can be in step or out of step with this cycle. I have at least the illusion that I was born at the start of another cycle, the beginning of the thaw, when Moscow came back to life after a thirty-year deep freeze.

Moscow in the sixties

My childhood was enveloped in the exhortative songs which were heard everywhere: from the loudspeakers on streets and from the "radio-point" – a concept which has disappeared into the mists of time: there were no transistor sets then and a piece of apparatus which sung, reported on football matches and read out all the parts in plays was plugged into a special radio-socket. But as I reached school age something new appeared: television. It was black and white with a small screen and the same old films were shown on it over and over again and the same bits of news about record-breaking dairymaids and miners' feats. On television you could see the people who had been singing on the radio. My Mum also used to sing – just for fun, at home, and I have always held on to the impression that the beginning of the sixties was a time when everyone wanted to sing. So as a result a new invention appeared: the tape-recorder. The first ones were large, unwieldy objects with bobbins, on which to wind the tape. My dad used to bring tapes home and they had completely new songs on them: songs sung by "bards", or minstrels, who also wrote the words. These singers were the ones who began to undermine the enormous graven image of the state, the machine which used people as its cogs. They brought in the fashion for the personal, which had up till then been qualified with negatives: bourgeois, petty, lacking class consciousness. The songs of the "bards" and popular songs had one thing in common, romance. In one song there was a 'morning tinting the walls of the ancient Kremlin with soft light, and the whole Soviet Union waking up with the dawn', in another the singer was 'going, going, going to find the fog and the scent of the taiga'.

This romantic mood was being added to all the time by new appearances. It wasn't just the wondrous new things being invented every day, the first person flying to the moon, the news of great feats of construction and unsurpassed harvests. The rates of productivity, which for some reason were compared with 1913, made everything seem bright. And Mum used to say, 'How lucky we are to live here and now.' But the more and greater our luck the more it turned into a duty. An American smile didn't work as a Soviet one, because it was demanded together with the threat of punishment, in the way that a frightening nursery school teacher demands obedience. Avant-garde artists appeared and scandals and controversies arose about them. Two writers were put in prison for publishing their books abroad and in Leningrad a poet was tried for 'parasitical behaviour',[1] that is, for not working anywhere. By the end of the sixties I realised that I hated the Soviet regime and all its pro-paganda: the songs, film, healthy Soviet families, workers, peasants and 'the fighters for world peace across the globe'.

Moscow in the seventies

In the seventies the illusion of Socialism with a friendly face came to an end and it began to seem as if this brutish regime would last for ever. A third wave of emigration began (the first was after the revolution, the second after the Second World War). But an even greater number of people went into 'inner emigration'. Students of the humanities attempted to concentrate on themes in the far past in order to avoid contact with 'that great leading force – the Communist Party' or turned to other countries: under the pretence of exposing 'rotten bourgeois ideology' writers at least attempted to say something about foreign art or philosophy.

---

1. The two imprisoned writers were Andrei Sinyavsky (Abram Terts) and Yulii Daniel'. The poet tried for 'parasitical behaviour' was Joseph Brodsky.

I also went into "inner emigration": we poets, artists, musicians (who were later called the 'second culture') met up in people's homes, where exhibitions were put on, evenings of literature and music were held, and contemporary life was discussed. We swapped *samizdat* and photocopies of different books, which were forbidden or hard to get hold of. These were, in fact, the most interesting books. We watched films at 'special showings' where to get in, one had to push a way through with someone who was allowed in. But this period, which might seem from the outside to have been unbearable, did have its pluses. The sweetness of the forbidden fruit engendered in us an enthusiasm for knowledge: my generation is altogether more educated than the ones that came before and those that came after. This is thanks to the appearance of photocopiers. Every book that got to Moscow (and they only went to Moscow, and then some of them on to Leningrad) was circulated in thousands of copies. So we had studied everything from Kierkegaard, Nietzsche, Jung and Steiner to Vladimir Nabokov and Roland Barthes.

Many studied foreign languages in order to read the texts, which weren't translated into Russian, or in order to leave. The previous Soviet generation was denied the opportunity to know things that weren't in the officially approved selection. The generations after us were trapped by laziness – when you have everything, you do what's necessary for work and the rest of the time you "get away from it all" – bars, clubs, restaurants, shopping, television, holiday resorts. There's no time and no energy for self-perfection, unpaid creativity or understanding the meaning of life. In the seventies there was the concept of '*netlenka*' (the 'incorruptible' or 'eternal'), which quickly became ironic – it meant everything that was done not for wage earning, but for "eternity": books written "under the table", films made "for the shelf " and pictures which could never be shown.

Another positive outcome was the fact that the circle of intelligentsia swam against the current of "pap for the masses" and sought an individual way of life – reading between the lines when reading the newspapers or listening to a hiss through which the barely perceptible voices of a western radio station could be heard.

At the beginning of the eighties the government increased its pressure and Bulat Okudzhava's [2] words gained relevance: 'Let's take each others' hands, friends, so we don't disappear one by one.' Moscow joined up with St Petersburg, the boundaries between the "official" and the "second" culture were fixed in stone, rock music and superficial pop became mutually exclusive, barricades were erected on all fronts. Then there was a breakthrough – Gorbachev began *perestroika*. The feeling of alienation was lifted from us – Moscow came to life: on the Arbat [3] young people sang songs, read poems, sold pictures, the first "cooperative" (or private) restaurants and boutiques appeared, people made pancakes outside on street stalls, fruit was sold directly from cars which had driven up from the South. Concert halls were filled to bursting: all the recent past's underground works could be heard in official venues. The mounted police were frequently called out to exhibitions, concerts and literature events, to stop the people who couldn't get in from storming the building. These were unprecedented times: there was a rapturous sense of unity, creative energy burst forth like a fountain, and our hope became a certainty that at last the good life was about to begin in Russia. And then the outside world was opened to us and we found that it loved us – and how we had adored it from a distance up till then!

During *perestroika* Moscow came to life, but it didn't get any more beautiful. Soviet Moscow had meant completely dark streets, derelict building fronts covered with a layer of dust and fumes. Sometimes they were painted in some awful 'soiled' (as people put it) colour. Awful, because that's what Soviet paint was, 'soiled' (a greyish-brownish-reddish colour) because they still looked stained and splattered. This painting made things even worse because they painted right to the top, over cracks, bubbling plaster, around the crumbling corners. Repair work was, to their mind, too expensive and unnecessary. There is such a phenomenon as 'making the ugly uglier'. If a block's entrance hall is horrible, with uneven walls, a lift like a coffin, and all of this covered with scribbled obscenities by kids and teenagers and gauged with knives, and then this is where drunks come to drown their sorrows and answer calls of nature... well that's it, no one wants to repair the building. There's no point

---

2. The dissident writer, poet and bard Bulat Okudzhava (1924-97).
3. Pedestrianised historical street in the centre of Moscow.

in decorating a little cage of a flat in a sixties block, or creating any comfort in it – it won't ever look any less like a prison cell.

If Moscow in the sixties danced and sang and Moscow in the seventies searched for knowledge and a means of survival, then Moscow of the eighties spewed up its long restrained feelings: hate, indignation, revenge. But on a personal level for a short while people grew so very close and found so much love for each other that there was an endless series of passionate affairs.

Moscow in the nineties

Moscow had its heyday in the nineties. In just a few years the old buildings were restored and we discovered that Moscow had architecture. The blocks of flats built during Khrushchev's era were pulled down and wherever possible buildings were repaired or given a new face. There was a great deal of new building work. Moscow became bright and alive twenty-four hours a day, fantastic shop windows and flawless office blocks appeared, roads were repaired and new traffic measures installed. We discovered too that Moscow wasn't an industrial site or a dump, but one of the most beautiful cities on the earth. It would be dishonest not to note that we owe all of this to the Mayor of Moscow, Luzhkov. In Russia 'the terrible' and 'the wonderful' are brought about not by general everyday efforts, but by sudden bursts of energy and individual personalities.

The majority of the Russian population is always and by turn discontented. Even those who used to criticise Soviet power were overcome by nostalgia: for the hundred roubles paid to those who worked and those who just clocked in at work, for the equal poverty and lack of freedom suffered by everyone except the "untouchables". They even began to miss the outlawing of the expression of discontent. And then this all of a sudden some had it all, others nothing – Wild West capitalism, devoid of almost any social protection. But for all that – freedom and the freedom to choose, to say and do as you please. The whole country began to hate Moscow. The capital became so much more beautiful and richer than other towns that it caused them offence. If there is a place where freedom is valued, it is Moscow. Moscow has so much to lose.

In 1989 one of the first of the democrats of Gorbachev's new wave, Yury Afanas'ev called the Deputies 'supporters of the tyranny of the aggressively obedient majority'. He didn't understand back then that he was talking about the majority of the Russian nation, still Soviet, which had no need for freedom and found inequality unacceptable. It is freedom itself which makes this majority aggressive and helpless, and the whip which makes it obedient. Moscow is the exception to this.

Back in the 18th century Karamzin wrote 'from the time of Catherine the Great Moscow has been reputed to be a republic. Without doubt there is more freedom there'. Moscow in 2000 is a city which is comparable with any western European state. Only the people are different, neither eastern nor western. If you ask them for help they will hear you out, help you, support you. In the last few years a number of foreigners have settled in Moscow, attracted by these warm, almost familiar relations between people. Of course you can also be taken for a ride, without apparent rhyme or reason. This is the "mysterious Russian soul" at work.

In spite of all the wars and revolutions there is an amazing sense of indestructibility in Moscow. The Ivan the Great bell tower inside the Kremlin has never been affected by any disaster and there is even a belief that whilst it stands Moscow will never fall. Red Square has witnessed many changes, but its paving stones and convex surface (as if to remind us of the earth's spherical nature) remains the unshakeable centre, the point of calculation and a symbol. Whilst Lenin's body stays, the masses, that is the nation which has not yet become a civil society, still rule the roost. Today a weariness of history, an understanding of the pointlessness of social shake-up has replaced romantic excesses. But Muscovites feel themselves to be in good health and more than ever rely on Providence, exemplified in the Russian proverb – 'if God doesn't provide, then the pig can't eat'.

Craze

Our country has always adhered to the "boom" model, and even now the western model of "evolution and catalogue" is tried and absorbed with the "boom" at its heart. When I returned to my country after a period of absence, I (as a typical citizen) was drawn into the games which 'all Moscow' was playing. In Paris people use the phrase 'all Paris' with far less restraint.

So, for example, in spring 1995 all Moscow was buying washing-machines. I had lived for five years in the West and never paid any attention to the type of machine in which I washed my clothes. But I had hardly arrived back in Moscow when an awareness of washing machines was thrust upon me: Aristons, Indesits, Boschs, with a laundry bag or without, frontloading or toploading, and half of my friends told me that they had bought a washing-machine the day before or that very day. There was a wave of enthusiasm. I bought a washing machine too and there was an end to the matter.

At one time that was exactly how productions at the Taganka Theatre were discussed, or émigrés and those who were forbidden to emigrate. Then there was rock music, trips abroad, and now there is the bourgeois and particularly the house-owning craze which has lasted a few years already. I was startled by the new word 'euro-decor'.[4] I had it explained to me and to start with I used to argue with it, saying there was no standard way of doing things in the West and not everyone even had their walls painted white, but of course it wasn't about the reality of the situation, but the myth, the boom in fundamentally changing your interior decor.

If you imagine the general style of our Moscow flats, it is, above all, an overload of objects: furniture, books, vases, trays, tea services, knick-knacks, Grandma's trunks, and everything else you can't bring yourself to throw away. The home used to be a warren where not just the important things were taken, but everything that might be of possible use to your grandchildren. So here the grandchildren are, and they've chucked out all the old tat, because the price of property is much higher that the price of the objects in it. It is probably true that there's a financial dimension to this change. For some time in the West property has had the highest

---

4. *Evroremont*, or 'eurodecor' is used to describe Russian flats with western style kitchens, bathrooms and white walls. During the 90s it came to mean all changes in interior decoration.

value of all: there isn't much space and a square metre costs more than the most expensive cupboard you could put in it.

Perhaps that's why people have started reading less – because a library is an unwieldy thing, a dust-collector, and it can't compare with newspapers, which you read and throw out. There is also the feeling, of course, that all the fundamental things have been read, and it's better to keep the *Encyclopaedia Britannica* on CD-rom. Moscow has become speedily computerised. And all the cockroaches have been speedily exterminated. As a result Moscow has left the kitchen, the quintessence of a warren. Anyone who could, tore down the walls to get rid of the two or three little cells and replace them with a sort of castle ceremonial hall behind a steel door, surrounded by the moat of an intercom system.

Fear, which reigned for so long in Moscow, had its last gasp over criminality and then disappeared and was replaced by ordinary cautiousness. The attraction of normality is also a novelty. Before, if you told someone they were mad it was a compliment, everyone wanted to be unusual. And now the task before us is to achieve some degree of normality. Achieving this standard of normality appears at the moment harder than getting blood from a stone.

In this way, too Russia is demonstrating its own style – from the West's everyday objects it manages to create a new adventure.

In Russia the most important thing is to avoid boredom. Even the simplest trip to the shops has to turn into an emotional voyage: no milk here, butter there, the shop that used to have meat doesn't any more, and another one does, but it's very expensive. You walk around, promenade at the same time and witness life. You have the time, but not the money. Then all of a sudden it's the other way round. In Paris, where I spent two years, I went into a local shop and bought everything in fifteen minutes. I was in ecstasy for a while, because this simple operation had been performed against the backdrop of the Arc de Triomphe. Then I got used to it. It is impossible to get used to Moscow. Something is being built, rebuilt or repaired all the time, and yesterday's dirty old pile is today's luxury manor. Of course, at some point in the past the luxury manor was turned into a dirty old pile. But in this way change is constant and it is never boring, there is always a new craze. Even nightclubs – you'd think a disco was a disco, but all of a sudden they too were a phenomenon. Whilst the boom lasted everyone was drawn to them: the beau monde, celebs, even poetry readings took place in nightclubs.

In Paris you live to the measured sound of wheels and everyone has the timetable in front of them. But no one has worked out where Russia is heading and whilst you ask the questions life continues.

Essays inspired by *The World of Perceptible Things in Pictures*
by Jan Amos Komensky, exhibited at the Pushkin Museum of
Fine Arts to celebrate the tercentenary of the publication in 1997

Wayfarer

Because I am a follower of subjective realism, I am familiar with
my wayfarer. He is a person upon whom pictures impress them-
selves more than numbers, his discoveries take place in the urban
jungle and not in the wilds of scholasticism. This wayfarer has
never been a Talmudist or a dogmatic follower of the text. He loves
rum, the stars, his favourite pictures are detailed, many-coloured
maps and *Michelin* guides. He is a seafarer and a lover of fast cars.
He is Columbus, who discovers America for himself, because for a
long time people haven't stuck to their own parts of the globe, white
people knowing nothing about red people, or yellow people about
black people. Now we have come together and each one of us is
searching for paths, by himself and for himself. My friend, the
wayfarer was looking for them in the symbiosis of books and sex.
Now he looks in travel agencies. The age of great geographical
discoveries on a different level has begun.

Clearly my wayfarer has no family. Who would want to drag a
wife and family through tempests! Unlike the *sedentaire* this wayfarer
does not try to digest the world in some order – starting with our
Egyptian ancestors, moving through the Greeks, Romans, Israelites
and onto the Gauls, Celts and Russians, for example. He's impatient,
he can't wait for the centuries to do their thing. Or perhaps he
doesn't have the vision within to pick out the pyramid, poisonous
snake, medieval fortress and cliff-face hieroglyphics in his genes.
He needs a picture, but not a film shot by somebody else, and his
own spyglass to give it taste and smell. In fact, in this exoticism,
this foreignness, he is looking for himself, but in such a random,
unmediated way that he is utterly uninterested in the ancient
sakura, yet responds keenly to the chattering of the jackals in the
baobab groves.

I am also a wayfarer, but a different sort. I am drawn to goats and camels, gothic cities and the Atlantic Ocean. Still, one wayfarer understands another better than he does the people who live according to collective common sense. And that's from our earliest childhood. We always had top grades for geography – but we can't work out where they extracted their square roots from.

[1997]

The World

Some people say it's a small, intimate world, others that it's huge. In fact everyone draws their own map. On my map the centre of the world is Europe and it has two capitals: Moscow and Paris. France is taste, conceived and trained to perfection, temptation and the immortality of the flesh. Russia is the wilderness which can't be wiped out, where history's eventful progression is constructed out of mirages. And in the middle there is a fortress: Moscow. There I seek my defence. But one must also be something of a fighter. Moscow gives strength and demands toughness. In Paris one must be soft and processed, like a purée.

Europe is washed by oceans, refreshing it with African passions, Persian cats, Arab stallions, Chinese restaurants, Indian incense and Japanese aircon. On the other side of the ocean live the Indians. They wear jeans, drink coke, eat burgers, and they have feathers growing on their heads. But because wanderers from all corners of the world roamed their way, they built a new Babylon, a much loved mingling-place for city dwellers.

There are villages, too, where the world is drawn up along verticals: from the sky to the ground, the ground to the sky, passing through roofs of red brick, black tar, shingle, straw, through wooden frames, planking, daubed-wood cottages, through cupolas and domes. Every well under its own moon. Every vegetable has its season: a time to sow the seeds, and a time to gather the fruits. Only milk, milk is constant, reflecting the essence of our Galaxy, of the Milky Way. Although I cannot get used to the fact that we see it – that is ourselves – from the outside. It's as if this is because we are twisting ourselves round into a spiral, and so everything in our lives appears to be the same, although it isn't. Still I'd like it if there wasn't any bad at all, and the good remained just as good. Or if we could gaze at the bad from outside, standing within the good.

But because it doesn't happen like that, we rush around madly making the world more varied, and saying to ourselves, 'We need variety in things, variety in people is most important...variety, yes, that's it, blue and red...' We think of ourselves as alchemists, capable of turning quantity into quality.

[1997]

State and Country

It might appear that state and country are different things. And that 'country' is a good thing, whilst 'state' is a bad thing. From the point of view of a citizen with long experience (former USSR, Russia and on a virtual level, or as they used to put it, in one's soul, France), I tell you there is no difference.

A king, five republics, socialists in power, right-wingers in power ...and nothing has changed. The same elegant taste, instinct for beauty, head for temptation. The same Derridas and Descartes, Tartuffes, Harpagons and the same Nostradamuses. The unthinkable in Russia: 18th-century houses, preserved through all the coups and wars all across France, solid and well maintained – and people live in them. Not a feather has fallen from Versailles, not a stone from Notre-Dame.

'In the management of state one should find a use for everything and never neglect that which may prove useful' (Richelieu). 'When the majority of people dream of glory, then the state will flourish and find happiness. When the majority of people dream of wealth, then the state will perish' (Saint-Just). 'At the heart of all patriotism lies war. For that reason I am no patriot' (Jules Renard). 'Patriotism is good for Africans and Asians, but for Russians it is suspicious and in France it is a sort of madness. Advanced minds should dissociate themselves from patriotism' (J.M. Domenach). 'In order to make a country wealthy you must sow diligence into all hearts. In order to make a country poor you must sow despair

111

in them. The former is aroused by work, the latter consoled by laziness' (Montesquieu).

All Gogol's eccentricities: the corruption (including the offered bribe of Borza puppies), the Khlestakovs, the Akaky Akakieviches, the registration of dead souls, the pool in the middle of Mirgorod – it's all good and true, all Chekhov's languor, the yearning, felling of cherry orchards, provincial intelligentsia and boorish common sense – all good and true. Dostoyevsky's world – couldn't be more right. Esenin ('They sing again here, they fight and cry, remembering Great Rus' ') and Blok ('The Railway Line') – all good and true. Pasternak's 'Farewell to the years of timelessness' is timely at every point. Brodsky, too – 'The outcast of an untamed power with a smashed-in face' could not have been said by any Frenchman at any point in their history. Frenchmen sing 'Douce France'.

Russia loves tyrants because it is not a cohesive country. The spirit of opposition alone can overcome Russia's laziness and only then is the merciless state displaced – and then the whole thing starts again. The problem is emerging from the fairy tale, waking from Esenin's 'sleepy golden Asia, resting on cupolas', arousing lazy Ivan the Fool from his sleep on the warm stove, getting rid of Oblomov. In France the opposite is true: they could do with some dreams and aboriginal might.

[1997]

Outward and Inward Feelings

In outward feelings acquisition prevails, in inward feelings loss does. When I am on my own I think about having lost my mother. Life goes on and on as if it were eternal, and yet while it passes, people never manage to reach out to each other. Everything shoots off at tangents, some pleasant, some less so. All of it shrouding some or other essential truth, which is never quite revealed. And then – all at once – there's an illness and that's it, it doesn't matter what else is going on, suddenly we discover we are mortal. No more life. Neither the tangential sort, nor the 'reaching other people' sort. There's nothing. However, the presence of something or other isn't excluded. Still to the naked eye – nothing.

Yet when addressing the outside world I cover my lips with an exultant smile by Christian Dior and my eyes wear the animated gleam they have worn from childhood. Everyone is delighted with my endless acquisitions – the fax, for example: 'At last! At last we can write to each another quickly, more often, more easily!' But we write exactly as much as we did before. We write when we need to. And socially, well there is the pleasure of a meeting, even if it is a matter of circumstance. A rush of emotions regarding new purchases, *haute couture* suits and fashionable slippers – never glass ones.

On my own I think about having lost love. I don't know why, really – it's hardly a pair of gloves mislaid absent-mindedly. Nor is it a lack of desire or enthusiasm. It's something else.

And all the time we look on and delight in acquisition: creative successes, the discovery of new countries, the awarding of honours of every sort.

On my own I think about having lost my son – not the person, but one's continuation, not generally, but for oneself. And actually that was a lack of enthusiasm and an absent-mindedness. Where did the absent-mindedness come from, I ask myself? Karma or something? Because it was written into my stars at birth? I don't know whether that should make me feel better or not.

Outwardly I'm so upbeat that unobservant people often ask me, 'Are you always so pleased with things?'

[1997]

The Providence of God

'...a world departing into darkness, where we knew to whom we did the evil that we did' – JOSEPH BRODSKY

We know about it from the countless centuries of history, which have pulled up sharp against our palpably real 1990s. A soldier is killed in war. Men are killed in duels. Galileo is tortured for the insult done to humanity. We cannot let this insult pass, because it is vitally important that we have ground beneath our feet, firm ground, the steadiness of that upon which we stand. And if we're standing, then we're standing and not revolving. They burnt Giordano Bruno and it's clear why they did that, too. Being anthropocentric, it was difficult for us to come to terms with a plurality of worlds and an infinite universe. Man was the measure of all things. Woman was not a person. They used to call women witches and burn them. That was what it was like then: the church exterminated those with whom it considered it difficult to come to an agreement. And it's hard to come to an agreement with women. That's how Stalin operated, but being from the Caucasus he wasn't scared of women. So all in all, tyrants, vendettas and feuds. And everyone knows why they crucified Jesus.

Then all of a sudden there are no heretics. You can say what you like. Humanity's worth and honour cannot be insulted, there is no more coercion, no slaves and no colonies. Just freedom and legislation. And the loss of leadership. Terrorists operating like blind fate, bomb blasts killing chance passers by. And if we knew once that war was war, now there is no more war, no more peace. There's Rushdie writing away, writing, and all of a sudden some strangers in a foreign country sentence him to death. They offer a large reward. They increase it to an enormous size. And what if one of the people hiding the writer wavers? That is what he lives with. Terrorism increases in strength, sects increase in strength, maniacs increase in strength and number. And no one can say anything. Only nonsense, if the nerves can't stand it – answering with something along the lines of the war in Chechnya. What about trying to root out the terrorist? He isn't even hiding. He's not a real person – he grows and increases by limb division. Put one in prison for an explosion and ten more appear. We can discuss it, grieve over it, feel indignant – but we can't stop it. The maniac needs to kill – one wants to kill children, another whatever he can.

It seems likely that this is the providence of God. Possibly providence also grants things in the same way – to the ordinary group of passers-by. Still, now it's difficult to remember when and where that was.

[1997]

A Game of Chance

The game of chance is a game of geography: stopping in the so-called right place at the right time. So you stop. 'The postmen have aged, the addresses have long since changed' and you're left standing there like a fool.

I've heard that it's all about 'relationships'. How they worked out, didn't work out, went cold, sour, pear-shaped. And it can happen in different ways: a meeting on holiday, buying the same sort of dogs – and friends for life. Although if the holiday ends or the dog dies, the friendship dies with it.

I had a friend M. At first he was in love with me. He offered me his hand, his heart and other organs. I wasn't so attracted by the other organs, I liked his soul. I fell in love with the organs of another M, yet became bosom pals with the first M. He, unlike me, knew that my affair would finish when one of us moved, and he waited. Waited and once again found out that I'd take his soul, but not his organs. But because he had no loved one in his life anyway, I was better than nothing. So we were friends, ringing each other up everyday, seeing each other once a week, exchanging letters when on holiday. It was an fool's paradise – brothers forever. But as soon as M found the love of his life he threw me out of it.

I had another bosom friend, Vesian. My return to Moscow archived the file of our friendship, and it remained a completely Parisian one. But my friend Mitya remains a friend because, although he moved to Prague, he has free use of an office phone and he has to come to Moscow from time to time. I had a friend Olga in St Petersburg and even then I had calculated that 650 kilometres was the limit on distance in a friendship. So there is it, the whole game of chance. My love 'unto the grave' for the other M dried up slowly and disappeared according to the distance of separation.

I'm very sorry that they have all disappeared. They probably replaced me with others, as if in each person there were flowerbeds which had to be sown with something, this year carrots, next year roses – there's a game of chance here, too – whatever comes to hand is planted. 'I wanted to buy seedlings or little strawberry plants, but nothing to wrap them in...so got the dill seeds instead...'

It's said that one old friend is better than several new ones. I like old friends best – vintage, seasoned, with a taste of oak barrels. Not an immature sour-green.

So that's why chance doesn't enter into a game with me. To me, my neighbours are no closer than that remote, dried up and maybe expanding figure, bursting with the blood of my heart.

[1997]

Temperance

Temperance is the 14th arkana in Tarot. If you are looking at it, then it has already fallen to you. A girl-angel pouring water either into a jug or from a jug. It is an ambivalent card. When it comes with the Fool it means defeat, with the World it means success. By itself it is only positive in the sense that 'no news is good news'. Not much help if you're waiting for news. If it comes with Judgment, Temperance brings closer the moment when one stands before the mysterious Day of Judgment, yet delays the impatiently awaited moment of receiving. Beside the Lovers it can mean the passage to marriage, and also the extinguishing of love. Golden mean or golden mediocrity? Even the ancient Romans asked themselves this question.

It is an optimistic card. It means an end to torment. But it is also a pessimistic card if you are hoping for a miracle. Temperance is a breathing space, a settling tank whilst waiting for fate. Except for the spiritually enlightened, for whom Temperance is fate.

Temperance suggests relying on one's own resources. Papus said about it: 'Son of Earth, measure and test your strength, not so that you can retreat from a deed, but in order to destroy obstacles, in the way that water, drop by drop, sharpens stone.' Eteila sees it as advice 'to use everything in moderation' in order not to lose it all so soon. M. Moran plays for higher stakes: 'The card Temperance symbolises the connection between the visible and invisible worlds, and causes us to think about the reversibility of all movement: liquid can flow in one direction as well as in another.'

So is the water pouring into or out of your jug?

Temperance was never better expressed than it is by this scrap of time at the moment. When no one wants major shocks, no one stakes everything or puts their faith in tomorrow, no one spends their last on a good time, or allows themselves to be carried away by reckless passion. Little is taken for granted, everyone is finding meanings for things, for themselves first of all. It is a time of settling debts. Sobriety, self control, restraint, economy, caution – only then will the correct circulation begin, the necessary will flow in and out.

It is vital to use the gifts of Temperance, because the next card, the 15th arkana, is the Devil, and then there will be no more indulgence. No time to think – it will be all fate, passion, violence, lightning flashes, the desire for power and captivity. If you haven't managed to catch your breath, to prepare, find yourself a layer of resistance – well, you may find yourself being fried in a pan. Those who have drunk from the cup of Temperance are better defended than the others.

[1997]

Water Birds

Every life is linked with them: the swan, sandpiper, heron, duck.

I remember a Russian riddle from my childhood: Who is in the marshes crying, but won't leave? Answer: the sandpiper. The riddle made a lasting impression on me: I squeezed out the sandpiper in me – not drop by drop, but all at once and for half my life. I never cried in the marshes. If I didn't like something, I left. For example, I didn't like the Soviet government, and neither did I like dissidence or emigration. I always, always found somewhere I could leave for. However, my pride didn't last long. I was caught up in a pine tree and became a sandpiper. So I do understand them. I also understand the heron. How it rises above the sandpipers, the marsh, hovering regally. One might ask where on earth it's going. Of course it's no pink flamingo – the ones that pose in clans in beautiful landscapes – just a lonely heron, standing on one leg, with the other serving as a TV aerial.

There have been times when they have started building cities on marshes – Moscow, St Petersburg. The capital – and round it frogs are croaking and it seems indecent that the heron is holding a naked bird in its long beak. So some hissing aspirin-type tablet is thrown into the water and it becomes a clear pool. And everything changes. Queenly swans float around, black and white, Odile and Odette, all very prestigious. If anything happens there is a public protest: 'Don't shoot the white swans!' Ducks are swimming alongside at the same time, modest girls and the brilliant males. You wouldn't know where to point the gun first on a duck hunt. There's nothing better than duck at a banquet. In extremely expensive restaurants the ducks are numbered and each one has been brought up individually, well looked after, fed on special food – they never feed swans like that. That's because pleasing the stomach is far more important than pleasing the eye. In embarrassment at this home truth, the phrase: 'The ugly duckling turned into a beautiful swan' was written into the theory of evolution.

After emerging from the egg the duckling takes the first moving object it sees to be its mother and follows it. For that reason there are no orphans amongst ducklings. They are the happiest of all mortal things: they swim, fly, walk on the ground, never cry and quack in a self-contented way. Strangely enough, though, no human being has ever admitted to envying them.

[1997]

Carriages

My transport history began with a tricycle. I managed to get as far as the water pump and then turn onto the squelchy path which led to the overgrown pond. Grandad once went in up to his waist in slime with a net to catch me some newts, of which I was very fond. I thought that other people would catch me newts too, so I changed my seat in a faded orange Zaporozhets[5] for one in a dark blue Lada, then from a Volkswagen Passat turbo diesel to a black Ford Escort. I tried a passionately dark-green Jaguar, but still I boiled with desire for the burgundy Lancia Thema. I boiled like a kettle with a piercing whistle to attract attention, but once I boiled dry, I realised that the tricycle was in fact the best vehicle for dispatching the cult of the Beautiful Woman. And the rusty wheelbarrow in which Grandad carried seedlings, fertiliser and me about the plot of land which belonged to an estate, was, however strange it may seem, more comfortable than the celebrated Mercedes.

Of course the type of carriage determines the destination. The best goers in my garage are the A-310, Tu-148, Boeing, IL-86. Once upon a time I spent my life on the 'Red Arrow'[6] train – now I've repainted the train. Lighting my way ahead with the flaming letter 'M' on a pole,[7] I am transported in a blue locomotive around Moscow's subterranean world. And although population density down there is in excess of usual hygiene standards, there's a green light ahead of the blue coaches.

In my garage there are no motorcycles, scooters, nor ponies and traps, as I don't go to the big markets and wholesale warehouses. But there is a little box which I use everyday as a lift, and sometimes outside in the open air – on the principle that Mohammed doesn't go to the mountain when he can take the funicular. I do occasionally link up with the lines of electronic communication via the trolleybus, but it's so unwieldy that a whole half hour passes, getting it out of the garage. I don't have a bus, or a tram, but there was once a river-bus, and you could ride it up the Moscow River. Now I don't have time for rides: I work like a beast and fly like a bird. Nothing human remains. The carriages are too many.

[1997]

---

5. Bottom of the range Soviet car, frequently the butt of jokes.
6. Prestigious train which travels between Moscow and St Petersburg.
7. Street sign indicating Metro station.

Trade

It's clearly best to trade in forbidden fruits. Drugs, people, children, passports, privileges. Still, it was probably not with this in mind that Voltaire wrote: 'the country with the greatest freedom in trade will always be the richest and the most flourishing'.

On the one hand the greater the taxes and duties, the less the freedom. On the other, a whole flourishing town was once built from taxes alone. Two monks barricaded a road and stopped all the salt traders travelling along it with the hardly god-fearing words: 'Pay or you can't pass.' That's how they collected money and built Monks town, München in German. Of course the price of salt in neighbouring regions went up because of the monks. But the population was quickly pacified when the cassock-wearing businessmen of Munich began brewing a secret monastery drink – beer, and began selling it to people. Cheaply. They called the beer 'Spaten', or 'spade', because the monks were always walking around with spades and building. Spaten is what they still drink now in Munich and good health to them.

V.I. Dal'[8] gives two Russian proverbs in his dictionary. On good trade: 'Better to trade than to steal', and on bad trade: 'Better to steal than to trade.' Theft is barter at the end of the day. I steal cucumbers from my neighbour's garden, he steals apples from mine. So then I poison my neighbour with cockroach powder and he poisons me with insecticide. Money passes hands to avoid an argument. But legalised trade often also has a godless element to it, yet this doesn't stop it being an engine of progress.

[1997]

---

8. Editor and compiler of a famous Russian dictionary.

City

The city beckons: it leads you out of the sweet silence into the crowds, exhaust fumes, smog, noise. Or you're on a ship, sailing, and in the evening the tiny lights of a city glimmer in the distance – just a city, even an unknown one, and the heart contracts and the city beckons.

The quintessence of the city is the megapolis, the capital. Where people kill, where those without compassion ruin life: arrogant Narcissuses and hidden maniacs. We are particularly attracted to it. To survive there – I mean here – where we are, is a victory for the newcomer. But as for us, we don't give a toss, a monkey's, a fuck or a fig for the lot. There's popular Moscow wisdom for you.

Tourists love both the big cities and the little ones which are marked with a star in the guidebook. Three stars means a big hit. More and more towns are becoming big hits. Maastricht because of a united Europe, Shengen because of the visas, Khasav'yurt because it's the end of the war in Chechnya. Seattle, because it's the place where two famous film plots take place. Delft, because it's Vermeer's town, covered in tiny bridges. Grenoble is the skiers' Mecca. Salzburg, because it's a Mozart heritage site. München is the birthplace of 'Heil Hitler', Nürnberg of 'Hitler's End', Vienna for the fairytales of Viennese coffee, forests, waltzes. Sidi-Bu-Said is the blue and white city.

The town of Po is where Henry IV was born and consequently the rooms in the customs house are oval, presumably because the future King was trying to invent his own designer style. Still, Ludovic won out on the world market. Dijon is the capital of mustard, blackcurrant liqueur, and the capital of Burgundy as well – that is, the best wines in the world. In Suzdal'[9] they give you mead to drink.

There is a tiny town in Holland, Oudewater, famous for the fact that during the Inquisition the only honest "weigher" of alleged witches lived there. All the others weighed the people and wrote down that they apparently weighed less than five kilos – and that sent them straight to the pile of faggots. But this honest man wrote down their real weight and the certificate was an Indulgence. Now they weigh tourists and give them a medieval style certificate of

---

9. Ancient Russian town and heritage site.

their weight, stating that they are not witches. Of course not all tourists want a certificate of how much they weigh. There is also Macondo, The Invisible City of Kitezh, Fooltown,[10] Mykhosransk. So it's not all roads by a long way that lead to Rome.

[1997]

Home

People who have always had a home and those who have never owned one have no idea of its qualities. The home is a labyrinth. I mean it's a constantly spreading, inexhaustible space, however small the flat. The internal eye multiplies every square centimetre of living space into specks and dents (or heroic feats of DIY) right up to the dimensions of its history. You'll never manage to find your way to all the bits, pieces and papers in your home. From time to time in one of the nooks and crannies – cupboards, on shelves, behind the cooker, the radiator or the fridge – you are amazed to come across some piece of rubbish. It might be the button from a long-forgotten dress, and immediately you remember everything: the dress itself, the circumstances in which you wore it, sewed it, bought it, threw it away. The dress was a whole era, and the sign of its end was the loss of this button, which has suddenly resurrected itself out of the dust.

There are treasures on the shelves: Christmas tree decorations in their prehistoric boxes, and here I found Mum's letter from the maternity hospital, telling Dad that I had been born. Those were the first words about me. There is so much drama in an battered old suitcase of letters. It has become, now that none of the addressees are still living, an exercise for the nervous system. But back then they had eternity stretching out before them, and none of them knew how it would end or what would comfort their heart. They suffered. I, knowing the outcomes, look at the bubbling power of them, like I might at a fire in the fireplace.

---

10. Glupov – the name given to Saltykov-Shchedrin's caricature of a provincial Russian town.

The imperfections of my own home do not bother me. They're mine. Other people's imperfections annoy me. In a rented flat there are no corners, curves, secrets. It is obvious what lies where. Everything is as clear as an open field. And it's like an official space, or an unpleasantly historical one: here's the table where some strange man ate his pound of salt, the bed, where some strange woman writhed around.

But I like hotels. Living in a space which is no one's. It's like flying into open space. You leave the unwieldy part of you on the ground and limit yourself strictly to the simple body, the functioning soul. Novelty excites, as if one was brand new to the world.

At home I have also introduced novelties. I have achieved my ideal bathroom. So now I can claim boldly, as Flaubert did, 'The bathroom is me!'[11] In the age of computers this is how handwriting manifests itself – the hand picking objects and placing them around the home.

[1997]

A Warm Room to Sleep in

Stars gaze into all rooms. Apart from the ones where there are bedbugs and cockroaches, where it's cold, and a washstand with cold water dripping into a rusty basin makes it colder. Where the stale smoke from a filterless cigarette hangs in the air; the smell of fag ends in an aluminium ashtray mixed with the scent of unwashed sheets fills a host of bottles on the floor – that's the only place where warmth collects, but the stars avert their gaze from that sort of stinking warmth, Ole Luckoie. Still if you open the frontier point, the window, and out of it there are lilac trees and a breeze then the most curious star will look in. Of course, it'll probably be some very cold star, but the inhabitants of one-star-rooms will tremble at the sight of it and busy themselves, squashing the bugs and throwing them overboard, together with the fag ends.

You need strength of will to attract the second star. And the

---

11. Flaubert is reputed to have said of Madame Bovary, 'Emma, c'est moi.'

third one, well, the hardest thing of the lot is required: feelings. Any will do: dignity, love, beauty. A feeling for baths, TV sets, balconies, where on a summer's morning three stars are reflected in the coffee: Vega, Altair, Deneb.

To progress to four stars you have to live a little, gain solidity. Pure romanticism isn't enough to set up a four-star flat or take a room in a four-star hotel. Or rather, the romanticism here is a stage already passed through. Four stars look down at people who are weary, a little disillusioned, but continue to feel and therefore to commit deeds. The deed gives form to the meaning of life. Heightened comfort is a surrogate for love. The fourth star took on the role of a support when the Summer Triangle – Vega, Altair and Deneb – announced its illusoriness: 'We stars are alight, but we give no heat and, if the clouds thicken, no light either'. The fourth star heats and lights as if to order, like an artificially fertilised egg, implanted wherever you request it. The four stars assemble for those who can order them. But the fifth star is for those who command. The commanding ones have become so weak that they need constant supervision. It's as if they're falling to pieces and every single piece must be cared for separately, so it doesn't fall off altogether. Five stars should bring atrophied organs back to life, turn on the erotic channels, feed the patient on a pulpy mass of black caviar and straighten the pillows. You might think it would be so hot with five stars that they would set you alight, but to the organism gradually getting colder this is just a warm room to sleep in.

[1997]

The Family Unit

The practical working of the family unit is something akin to the speaking of a language. You can't just pick it up. There's no 'taking to it' like a duck to water. Even a break in practice has a bad effect. You forget words and it becomes a real effort for other people to hear you out.

The family cycle begins with great-grandmother. She certifies the authenticity of the family relics and bequeaths grandmother her life, but not all of it, just the part spent in the family unit with great-grandfather. What went before that always remains a completely personal matter.

Then, like in the Tale of the Enormous Turnip, Grandma pulls Grandpa, Grandpa pulls the turnip, the rest of us tag along, and the family's genetic development sets off on autopilot.

In the summer at the dacha we all assemble for teatime. Grandpa has already earthed up the peonies, he carries the spade back to its place, changes his overalls for a pair of trousers and a white shirt, takes off his sunhat and combs his hair neatly. I picked strawberries in the morning and Grandma is already taking the basin of jam off the primus stove. By it, on a saucer, is the pink froth, my favourite treat. Mama has just finished sewing a white cotton sarafan covered with flowers and butterflies upstairs on her old Singer, and is now getting dressed for tea. Grandpa's woodwork bench is also upstairs, and up there amongst the pale curls of shavings from his plane you can find many curious things. Once I found a silver Moser pocket watch. It was broken. I did some magic on it and it started up again. Everyone said that they'd always told each other I was a genius of a child. In a good family that's how it should be. In every next generation the children are better than the parents, at least a little, because correct and careful genetic blood circulation means our ancestors live in us *en masse* and feed us. The autopilot held out for three generations before me, squeaking with the overload, breaking under the endless, echoing winds of the hurricane of revolution. The family's roots broke up on me. But I haven't got to that bit yet, I'm returning to the tea party from the forest in a fury. I'd been sent for a walk with a guest, a distant relative and a medical student who caught a frog (frogs and newts were my friends at this point), took a strange object called a scalpel out of his pocket and cut the little frog in half in a hideously enthusiastic attempt to show me how frogs are built. We never invited that student back.

So at last everyone is sitting around the table on the large open veranda. We have honey from the neighbour's beehives, froth from Grandma and me, a teapot on a Villeroy and Boch teapot stand belonging to my great grandparents. Here it is, the stand. It's almost the only evidence that I once belonged to a family unit which had survived from the creation of the world right up to our time.

[1997]

Medicine

There are two types of doctors: saviours and murderers in white coats. Often they are one and the same person: first they find the key to it all, then they make a mistake...Then they perform a miracle...but medicine is powerless...

I have a friend who is a hospital doctor. Once he told me as a secret that he had accidentally killed a little child – he had mixed up the bottles and injected the wrong medicine. No one guessed. They thought that the little child had died of its own illness. But that was just one case – the doctor saved all the other lives in his care.

The important question is the rightness of the intervention, taking the responsibility upon oneself for another's life. It's easy to say 'don't do any damage'. You have no chance of doing damage if you don't do anything.

My mother felt something wrong in her head for about fifteen years. She hassled the doctors, forced them to send her to hospital for tests, told them she'd had a stroke, she had brain disease, in short, she said everything she knew on the subject. But the doctors wanted to send her to a psychiatrist. And it was only when it became all too obvious that something wasn't right they did a scan and discovered a brain tumour. 'Too late to operate,' said the neurologist. 'If only we'd found it fifteen years ago.' But they did an operation anyway. A success. Two years after the operation my Mum put that surgeon on a pedestal. He became the most important person in the world for her. He also became very attached to her. Then one day she couldn't get up. It turned out that the disease hadn't gone away. The surgeon, who had always said that he had completely removed the tumour, admitted to me that it had been impossible to completely remove the tumour, but he had hoped that in an ageing body the process would be slower. He did another operation and she got much worse. I was the only person left in my mother's consciousness and memory. I was struck then by the stamina of love, in this case, maternal love. When everything else fails someone, what is left is what lived in every cell.

In her bad condition she took against the surgeon, deciding that he must have done something wrong. Right to the very end he told me an untruth (or perhaps it's what he thought?): that the worsening of her condition was quite temporary. It was impossible to believe this, but I did all the same. My mother died in hospital and at the same time the surgeon unexpectedly died of a heart attack at work. He had been a strong and healthy man. The funerals were held on the same day. And I thought to myself that there was some connection in all of this, that the medical intervention into the brain, and maybe not only the brain, had in some way connected patient and doctor. I don't mean that surgeons always risk something, but no one knows where the border is, beyond which the doctor is interfering with fate.

[1997]

God

For a non-religious person, God is light.[12] Not a senseless light, nor
an unfeeling light, but a focused one, as if seen through screwed
up eyes, an evaluating light, one which warms, chills, and, most
importantly, won't let us forget. All the rubbish, everything you
wanted to rip into bits and burn like a rough draft...he reminds
you of it all before too long. How you hurt a fly, how you made a
child cry, and how you were hurt and others made you cry as well.
I have the impression that every day we have the unique chance
to act 'in the flesh', yet all of these actions float in this light like
very fine particles or photons. If you were to dilute these particles
in water you would get life. The water evaporates and once again
you have the concentrate, the ever-present sediment. Of course
it's not water you dilute it in, but secretions, secret liquids. The
red carpet is laid out across the stones and you walk along it dully
– that is life. Or maybe not dully. The stone is the same sediment,
but compacted and no longer able to float.

For us, the Christians, we have the Man-God and his Mother.
I wear a cross, I have an icon of the Mother of God by my bed-
side. I think that it defends me. But I don't really understand it, I
don't know for certain, and I don't even believe the ones who say
they do know. But I absolutely can't imagine God as a sort of boss,
whom you have to flatter, to whom you write complaints. I'm not
certain that priests are God's channels. I find the divine in bits
and pieces from the world of culture and in good people. For me
God is a glue, holding together the essence of things. A guide,
who patterns everything with veins like maps; a source of breath
and desire which is not expressed by any one organ – the desire
to imitate Creation and comprehend its Design.

[1997]

*   *   *

---

12. Shcherbina plays on the Russian word *svetskii*, which means both light
and society, and by extension 'secular'.

August

August. I'm not in the world yet, but I soon will be. This leads to a change in the life of my family. My grandparents return from China, where they had been working for several years, in time for the birth. They bring so much stuff with them that during my childhood the house was Chinese: lamps, vases, silk, velvet, pictures, clothes to last me the next ten years. As a result, once I discovered Chinese food and Chinese literature I preferred them to others. Their arrival from China was just the beginning of that eventful August: Great-grandmother died, Grandma had her first operation for cancer and, together with Grandfather, built a dacha for me. Mother ordered bookshelves for the flat and from birth I am subconsciously aware of the large library at home as mine and I connect my life with books. I live, I feel my need that someone should live just for me. This need is painful because it is insatiable. It is because Grandma lived eleven years out of love for me and through force of will alone – from the medical point of view it was impossible. She died in August and so my Golden Age came to an end.

Things always happened in August. Once a distant relative got in touch and came to the dacha with her son, a medical student. They sent me, a five-year-old lover of bees, newts and frogs, for a walk in the woods with the student. I instantly fell in love with the nice-looking boy and I decided to share my treasured world with him. I caught a frog and showed him how I could talk with it. 'Do you know what's inside it?' asked the student. I was breathless, expecting to hear something along the lines of the secrets of Creation. But the student got out a scalpel, sliced open my frog's stomach and was on the point of explaining to me where the intestines were and where the heart was. I screamed and raced headlong back home. The shock of this disappointment in love lent such conviction to my request that the medical student should not cross our threshold again, that it happened as I asked. This August encounter with a murdering doctor gave birth to a scepticism in me towards that humanitarian profession: being a doctor is so rare a gift, how can it be possible to find so many of them?

August. Back at the dacha again. Mum and Grandad just don't get on and so a wall is built down the middle of the house. Feeling embarrassed, I run from one entrance to another and not straight through as we did when Grandma was alive. I'm entering puberty,

Grandad drinks in desperation, his life is irreparably destroyed. Mum is constantly irritated and shouting. A woman comes to stay whom I don't remember seeing before or after that. She's about 40, possibly younger, and called Lena. She has a horsy face and thick black hair on her legs. She arrives with her husband, who is disabled. I sit with Lena in the garden. She seems nice and kind to me, and her horsiness and hairiness, I supposed, were just the signs of a hard life, the once beautiful Lena deformed. I ask her a question, something like 'how come someone as nice as you married someone so unattractive?' I don't yet realise how tactless this is. The answer she gave puzzles me now. I would have expected her not to have answered, to have snubbed me or said something nice about her husband. But she said: 'You can wait your whole life for a prince on a white steed and end up with something you didn't want at all.' It sounded very heartfelt to me.

Not at all what I thought – that everything would happen as I wanted it to. But I couldn't have imagined that my life would be filled with strange things, 'aliens' as they called them in the film of the same name. That which is one's own is favoured, chosen, becomes a part of oneself. The alien is like a strange body which lives inside you against your will, takes your form and finally rips you apart and destroys you. Lena was the first one to explain the alien theory to me, and later I encountered it more than once: random choice of study, random children, work you're forced to do, an 'other half' you didn't ask for – all in all, survival in the harsh conditions which parents placed you in when they forced life upon you. 'And what's left to me? I don't have a choice.' That August I realised what I needed to fear.

In August it's hard to distract people from sunbathing and the burst of activity around the apple harvest: apple charlottes, jam, pies, goose stuffed with apple. People with children or grandchildren prepare every August for the move back to town from the dacha, they buy white hair ribbons, textbooks, satchels, shoes. All the same there's no shortage of 'heroes': in August the tanks entered Czechoslovakia, in August they annexed the Baltic states, the Communist putsch took place in August,[13] it collapsed. In August 1999 a plan was put together to move Russia towards yet more changes.

August 2000 went one step further. Concorde, the aviation miracle, crashed, Pushkin Square, the most crowded place in the centre of Moscow was bombed, the super-submarine *Kursk* went down,

13. Communist putsch against Gorbachev's reforming government in 1991.

the most reliable plane, the A-320, crashed. The Ostankino TV tower, the tallest building in Europe, burnt down. Russia went one step too far and was reined in. To the world's 'we can do anything', came the answer 'not everything'.

September, which has remained in our lives as the beginning of the school year and the season, was, as the legend has it, the beginning of life on earth. So in Israel, where the calendar didn't start with the birth of Christ, but with the creation of the world, the New Year happens to be in September. This August we are preparing to see in 5761. So the fruit from the tree of knowledge of good and evil (the apple, as it's known), is in some ways a New Year gift. It would be better to see in the third millennium in a spirit of reconciliation.

Light

We have come very close to the light. We have learnt to build light wells and draw light up in buckets like water which was always in our power: drains, canals, channels, rain butts, watermills, dams. Water is ours, it belongs down here, you can touch it. It is the horizontal axis of life and light is the vertical. We see light, absorb it into our skin, and yet there's nothing to touch – just the illuminated object. It's as if one couldn't pour water into a glass, but only compare glasses: this one's wet and that one isn't.

Light is the God Ra, Helios, Sun, a lamp, candle, fire. It is in our nature to hunt light. But if sunlight is understood as a manifestation of the divine, electricity is imitative. We were able to create it as soon as we became atheists, or Gods ourselves, in order to gain complete control over our own light. But still we are full of complexes with regard to our own creations. Did we do it well? Can we control it? Will it have any unforeseen consequences?

The flame, after thousands of years, should have become unremarkable. Yet to this day the bonfire at night symbolises the forces of witchcraft, night life lit by electricity is said to cause damage to the health, the candle is the attribute of magicians and spirits and in candlelight children tell each other ghosts stories and adults tell fortunes. Bandits roam at night with torches and in moonlight the forces of evil are let loose, ghosts wander – mythological fears. And beyond the myth the cock doesn't crow, man doesn't cross himself and thunder doesn't roll. Or perhaps it does; only no one notices, like anything located beyond the field of myth.

Procured light (the domestic sort and not the light which is sent down by Sun-Helios in its most intense form: nuclear energy, openly called Uranus and Jupiter) is associated with comfort, lighting that is not general, but personal: when only your face is lit up or a few faces, but not everyone's.

The history of light's mythology is contradictory and so confused that the name 'Lucifer', 'the light carrier' has been ascribed to the King of Babylon, the planet Venus, Christ and even Satan. Light has seeped into our daily lives with words like 'lux' and (in Russian) 'light' society means secular society. And precious stones and metals are no doubt drops and scraps of light, frozen in some amazing way: gold, silver, diamond, ruby, emerald. Otherwise they would be no dearer to us than cobbles, ore and glass. Our towns become more and more brilliantly lit in darkness.

Light and radiance are, as before, things to strive for, and darkness is a warning against the all-consuming black hole, anti-world, anti-gravity. Flames and burning are high-tension, white heat, danger, bordering insanity, low chakras, base instincts, low thoughts, the underground flame (the eternal flame is underground in our domain). Zogar, the book of the Cabbala, is dedicated to light and how it traversed the various stages. Light comes to us from the Creator through stages. The idea of hierarchy is for us, as for animals, total, and all our representations of the divine are based on this. Our attempts to free ourselves from hierarchy are endless and unsuccessful: democracy, "people's power" and attempts to institutionalise justice and equality are built into this hierarchy. Some animals quickly establish themselves as 'more equal than others'.

However many Gods there are on Olympus, there's only one higher God, and even if there's only one God, there are those who are closer to him and those who are further away. Each time we, with our pride in overcoming, exclaim 'Let the flowers grow!' it means that we have just pulled up all the weeds for the *nth* time and we hope they won't grow again. The problem arises not in relation to the actual weeding out of harmful creations, but because we have to constantly divide the world into good and evil, demons and angels. Even the sun doesn't just light and heat us – it blinds, it burns. The higher its level of activity, the more lethal it is for living things. But without it there is no life at all. It is characteristic of us, that in all ontological thought and doctrine we instinctively perceive ourselves to be a "lower" life, imagining even unknown galaxies and hypothetical aliens as "higher" life forms.

Transparency

So what is man? He's been the slave of God, a "personality" and now he's an image. 'I' has drowned in the accumulating layers of information. It has become impossible to separate out I's dried remains from these layers and he has once again emerged as an "image", in other words, a hieroglyph, a recognisable sign. Image is almost the same as a epithet: Lionheart, Eagle-eye, Pockmarked, Cross-eyed, Karlson on the roof. There's a place in society for those who are inscrutable with regard to their "personal" life, that complicated, ambivalent, unstable area. One has to become a single clear statement, unique in its way. Prigov – he's the one who screeches like a hobgoblin, Brener is the one who defecates in public, Kulik fucks goats,[14] Mr Dupin is the one who can eat four dozen oysters one after the other, Danny deVito is the short fat one. Khrushchev is the one who banged his shoe on the table.

It turns out that the body is the most unwieldy object, and far too intricate in comparison with the 21st century's "image" – geometric shapes, a minimum of heavy, opaque materials (stone, wood) and as much glass and transparent materials as possible. Those buildings, which are already in existence are illuminated in order to give them an appearance of lightness and transparency.

All of this could mean that the digestion process – of the outside world, "official" history, "off the peg" history – which had to take place behind closed doors, is also over. It's as if we've come to the conclusion that our form is final – or temporarily final – and decided to remain with it. Entrails are no longer packed away but are left on display, from the Pompidou Centre to the mechanisms housed in a transparent case. The insides of a living thing are now visible with the help of a scan and writers and filmmakers describe them in popular works.

New American and European architecture is a sign, representing the transparent and fragile human population, which no longer lives on the earth, but in the air, on the 5th or 105th floor. "Hi-tech" design is minimalist: no enormous lampshade-cupolas, many layered chandeliers, endless quantities of little bits and personal tat, the documentary evidence of lived years. An object is just as suitable for single use as a syringe – used and thrown away. Dumps are over-

---

14. Prigov is a Russian performance poet and artist. Kulik and Brener are radical Russian artists.

flowing, everything that isn't recyclable is used by artists who build installations out of unloved and therefore animated utility materials mixed with the less obvious old serviceable objects: pipes and wires.

Transparency has progressed to the numerous variations of fly-on-the-wall television: people agree to live together for a month or so under the constant surveillance of anyone who cares to watch. And this of course harks back to a religious awareness – living and knowing that every moment you are visible to The Unsleeping Eye, and you must therefore make an effort in order to meet its expectations. What is expected of *Homo sapiens* is more or less the same in all religions. But what if you live unobserved? Doesn't it stop mattering how you live? In the TV version you are seen by people who observe you, either come to like you or don't, and then vote for you to be dropped (like dying, disappearing without a trace) or to remain.

The name of the show *Big Brother* is taken from Orwell. It is what he described as a nightmare and what is seen as a nightmare in totalitarian countries: the KGB on patrol, Big Brother never sleeping, being trailed, bugged, followed and then imprisoned and shot. And who could have known that tracing you from your bank cards would become normal and watching you from behind glass would even have become desirable and altogether the highest personal achievement is when the paparazzi follow you without let-up. Famous for at least fifteen minutes, as Warhol put it, is different from the classical notion of fame. Fame was earned doing or creating some barely possible, exclusive thing – now the famous are those who are seen by the greatest number of people most often. On the television, of course: living on the other side of a glass TV screen brings fame just from the simple fact of its being broadcast. The intentness of the observation is transformed into the "image" of the thing.

The last wave of celebrities were the supermodels, who had to appear with a ready-made image. All of it the best efforts of nature and the stylists. Creativity and creation stopped being real necessities and the idea of a register with which one could play became more relevant: I like you, but not you...And all this is defined not by abstract divine attributes, but by society, a census of names kept by the state.

Society has increasingly become a confederation of groups and not personalities. A unique personal deviation has stopped being informative or even of interest. Handwriting has disappeared together with the disappearance of personality. Soon people will have forgotten how to write by hand at all. But not long ago I discovered a strange thing: the choice of font on a computer is also a form of handwriting and graphology may soon be replaced by fontology. There is a group of people (I am one of them) who write in Times New Roman. Others write in the font *Mysl'* ('Thought') – actually a philosopher once sent me a text in 'Thought'. My Israeli correspondent writes in Ariel and Ariel, as you know, is the ancient name for Jerusalem. Imitation handwriting fonts are used only in cheap advertising. And the more fonts appear, the clearer we will sense the handwriting – not a personal style, but a group one.

The luminous, transparent world is not just an invitation by implication to 'Look at one another' or a statement that 'there is nothing secret (hidden, intimate, forbidden) in me'. It is also a signal to light, space, higher powers, to everyone, everything. 'Have a look! What do you think? Come and take it!' It is a confession as long as life itself, a complete medical check. But if nothing notices and recognises it, then we won't be able to hold this position of readiness for much longer.

* * *

Why I don't live in Paris

The question I am asked most frequently is 'Why do you live in Moscow?' When people used to ask this, they referred to my belonging to a social minority: my European orientation, my fluent French, my avoidance of vodka, bathhouses, organised hikes and tracksuits, my sensitivity to design. Their conclusions went like this: 'you're not one of us.', 'You're more like a Frenchwoman', 'It won't get any better in Russia', '*Paris vaut la messe*'. This aphorism sounded to me like 'Paris is worth visiting regularly'. Visiting, because it is the capital of taste, style, wine, cheese, oysters, snails, *galant* behaviour and self-regard. Now five years after my return from Paris to Moscow, people ask as before why I'm here. Things are better in Russia already, Moscow has become a European city and the women look more French than the French.

There were two stages to my life in Paris. I fell in love with France at first sight and decided never to part from it. "Higher powers" must have guided my feelings, because there's no other way of explaining why they gave me residency straightaway, a free flat came my way early on (its owner went to live in my Moscow flat), I got a scholarship, then a prize, they published me in newspapers and periodicals, organised paid readings for me and published two of my books. I should also point out that I found a place for myself easily in Parisian society, and that the "boorishness" (a topographical fact) which had persecuted me before, left me. I found my way in this Parisian landscape and came to know it better than the Moscow landscape.

I wrote in French from almost the very beginning. I made a very good friend. A circle of friends appeared as quickly as if I had been a born and bred Parisian. The quality of the male attention I encountered here was quite unknown to me up till then. Offers of hearts and hands came in thick and fast, and if I had accepted any of them then I could have tied my life much closer to Paris. But I went my own way and took up an invitation from a longstanding friend, whom I had met back in Moscow. In Paris, for the first time, I felt the meaning of the phrase 'I'm happy', which had up till then just seemed like a figure of speech – 'I'm happy' I said to myself. I was happy because I was walking in these streets, because French sounded so soft, I began to love going into the little corner shops, beautiful *magasins* and cafés, dining in restaurants, walking in the Bois de Boulogne and the Bois de Versailles.

Paris was not my discovery of the West. Before that I had lived in America and Germany, I had travelled a great deal. So it wasn't the comparison with a Soviet backwater which enchanted me. American Beauty didn't tempt me, in Germany I felt utterly foreign, but here – well, it got to me. But after two years of Parisian euphoria a second stage began. Left on my own I started to see very distinctly that I was not a Frenchwoman. Nor was I like the Russian émigrés, who read the journal *Russkaya Mysl'*,[15] looked out for news from the homeland, stayed with their own cliques, despising the "aborigines" (the whole of the Russian emigration shared this) and hating all the other Russian groups. I was different from these, my contemporaries, and from the younger people (the phenomenon of "emigration" had already disappeared for them) who had come to Paris to set themselves up "at any cost" and who did so.

I didn't have that or any other aim. And then, just at that point, Oliver Stone's film *Between Heaven and Earth* was released and I came out of the cinema in tears after the film. I felt myself to be a false Frenchwoman, because Russian history and the Russian language were more rooted in me. Yet no one here could respond to this, the ancient in me, and not just the personal. In Russia I never even noticed it. Another person, even someone who had felt something similar, would have paid it no attention, but my nervous system reacted with a depression. I started travelling to Moscow more and more frequently and returning without enthusiasm. In Paris I had a dramatic affair and you might say that was the reason for my flight to Moscow, although, as is often the case, that was just the outer expression of an internal drama. The "Higher Powers" which had nudged me to Paris nudged me back again. Although it still attracts me as before.

[2000]

---

15. Newspaper of the Russian emigration, based in Paris.

In the Grip of Strange Thoughts
Russian Poetry in a New Era

Edited by J. KATES with a foreword by MIKHAIL AIZENBERG

Russian's political revolution of 1990 set off a cultural earthquake of unprecedented impact. But there were tremors four years before. The whole country saw the cracks starting to appear which eventually resulted in the overthrow of the old system, and the collapse of the confining roofs of direction and repression.

This anthology shows how a new generation of Russian poets have responded first to that evolving cultural shift and then to the difficult freedoms of a new era. No longer constrained by bureaucracy or ideology, these writers are producing a new literature of great energy and diversity. Working in styles ranging from traditional to avant-garde to postmodern, they depict the cascading changes in Russian life and culture – through the most intimate details of private lives to the larger images of a nation forging a new path for itself.

The book includes work by over 30 poets, with facing English versions by some of the most distinguished translators from Britain and America. The poets include Gennady Aygi, Bella Akhmadulina, Mikhail Aizenberg, Tatiana Bek, Dimitry Bobyshev, Bella Dizhur, Arkadii Dragomoshenko, Sergey Gandlevsky, Elena Ignatova, Fazil Iskander, Nina Iskrenko, Bakhyt Kenjeev, Viktor Krivulin, Aleksandr Kushner, Yunna Morits, Vsevolod Nekrasov, Olesia Nikolaeva, Bulat Okudzhava, Olga Popova, Dmitry Aleksandrovich Prigov, Irina Ratushinskaya, Evgeny Rein, Genrikh Sapgir, Olga Sedakova, Tatiana Shcherbina, Elena Shvarts, Viktor Sosnora, Sergey Stratanovsky and Mikhail Yeryomin.

BILINGUAL RUSSIAN-ENGLISH EDITION
234 x 156mm   464 pages
1 85224 478 X   £12.95 paper
North America: Zephyr Press

EVGENY REIN
Selected Poems

Edited by VALENTINA POLUKHINA

Foreword by JOSEPH BRODSKY

Translated by ROBERT REID, DANIEL WEISSBORT
& CAROL RUMENS / YURI DROBYSHEV

Evgeny Rein is Russia's greatest living poet. Born in 1935, he belongs to that tragic generation of Russian poets who for decades went unpublished in the Soviet Union, and didn't publish his first book of poems until he was 49. One of Akhmatova's 'magic choir' of young Leningrad poets, he was Joseph Brodsky's mentor and lifetime friend. Brodsky figures in many of his poems, and Brodsky's essay on Rein introduces this selection:

'Rein is unquestionably an elegiac poet. His main theme is the end of things, the end, to put it more broadly, of a world order that is dear – or at least acceptable – to him. The incarnation of this order in his poetry is the city in which he grew up, the city of Leningrad...

'But in contrast to the dramatic effect usually found in elegiac poets...the death of the world order in Rein is accompanied by a vulgar ditty from the 30s or 40s. Indeed, for Rein's work – and in my view he is the most gifted Russian poet of the second half of the 20th century – the cadences of Soviet popular music from that era probably had a greater influence than the technical achievements of the best among the Russian futurists and constructivists...

'Rein not only radically extended the poetic vocabulary and sound palette of Russian poetry; he also broadened and shook up the psychological sweep of Russian lyrics. He is an elegist, but of a tragic stripe. Few among his compatriots would dispute the depth of the despair and exhaustion that darkens these poems...'

– JOSEPH BRODSKY

Poetry Book Society Recommended Translation
BILINGUAL RUSSIAN-ENGLISH EDITION
216 x 138mm   176 pages
1 85224 523 9   £9.95 paper

ELENA SHVARTS
'Paradise': Selected Poems

Translated and introduced by MICHAEL MOLNAR
with additional translations by CATRIONA KELLY

'Elena Shvarts is a miracle, believe me. Her poetry is the purest of creations' – BELLA AKHMADULINA

'This is an explosive book by a dark, free, northern spirit, a woman born in Leningrad in 1948 but not openly published there until 1989. Bulgakov and Tsvetayeva (and Angela Carter) would feel at home in her violently imagined townscapes and landscapes. 'Paradise' was Peter the Great's word for his newly established city, but in Shvarts' poems the place is everything from a 'glorious dump' to a 'Rosa mystica', a 'gulf of chiming bells' to a sky of crows like 'scraps of burnt archives':

> *A tram swooped up, flushed crimson,*
> *and quietly swallowed me, like a wafer.*

Jagged feeling irradiates the extraordinary *Elegy on an X-ray Photo of My Skull*, but she is capable also of an offbeat narrative pathos, as in *A Parrot at Sea*, where the shipwrecked bird talks and squawks on a plank – and we can read as much as we like into that – as long as it can, before the ocean claims it' – EDWIN MORGAN, *PBS Bulletin*

Each new generation has to reinterpret St Petersburg, the place, the culture and its significance for Russia. Shvarts' haunted and demonic city is nearer Dostoyevsky's than Akhmatova's or Brodsky's. Her poetry draws backwoods, Russian folklore with its cruelty, its religiosity and its quaint humour, into stone, cosmopolitan Petropolis. She brings out both the truth and the irony of Peter the Great's 'Paradise', celebrating and reviling her native city as a crossroads of dimensions, a reality riddled with mythical monuments and religious symbols. Despite the blood beneath its pavements, her St Petersburg also reveals traces of an angelic origin:

> *Black rats nest over the shining river, in undergrowth,*
> *They're permitted, welcome, nothing can ruin paradise on earth.*

Poetry Book Society Recommended Translation
BILINGUAL RUSSIAN-ENGLISH EDITION
216 x 138mm   160 pages
1 85224 249 3   £8.95 paper